U-BOAT War

By Timothy J. Kutta
Color by Don Greer

squadron/signal publications

(Cover) U-377, a Type VIIC U-boat, glides slowly past the hardened submarine pens at Brest, France in 1943 while another U-boat prepares to depart for a patrol. U-377 was under the command of Oberleutnant Gerhard Kluth.

If you have any photographs of aircraft, armor, soldiers or ships of any nation, particularly wartime snapshots, why not share them with us and help make Squadron/Signal's books all the more interesting and complete in the future. Any photograph sent to us will be copied and the original returned. The donor will be fully credited for any photos used. Please send them to:

Squadron/Signal Publications, Inc.
1115 Crowley Drive.
Carrollton, TX 75011-501010

Если у вас есть фотографии самолетов, вооружения, солдат или кораблей любой страны, особенно, снимки времён войны, поделитесь с нами и помогите сделать новые книги издательства Эскадрон/Сигнал еще интереснее. Мы переснимем ваши фотографии и вернём оригиналы. Имена приславших снимки будут сопровождать все опубликованные фотографии. Пожалуйста, присылайте фотографии по адресу:

Squadron/Signal Publications, Inc.
1115 Crowley Drive.
Carrollton, TX 75011-501010

軍用機、装甲車両、兵士、軍艦などの写真を所持しておられる方はいらっしゃいませんか？どの国のものでも結構です。作戦中に撮影されたものが特に良いのです。Squadron/Signal社の出版する刊行物において、このような写真は内容を一層充実し、興味深くすることができます。当方にお送り頂いた写真は、複写の後お返しいたします。出版物中に写真を使用した場合は、必ず提供者のお名前を明記させて頂きます。お写真は下記にご送付ください。

Squadron/Signal Publications, Inc.
1115 Crowley Drive.
Carrollton, TX 75011-501010

Acknowledgements

Special Thanks: Shark Hunters International, Harry Cooper, Kaycee Cooper, Martha Ramponi, Susan Pence, Greg Spahr, Charles F. Coffey III, Lori Hawke, Andrew Hull, Richard Schmitt, Jeff Grissinger, and Jerry L. Wolfe.

All photos are courtesy of Shark Hunters International unless otherwise indicated.

Shark Hunters International is an organization dedicated to the collection, preservation, and dissemination of information on submarines. Shark Hunters has been in existence since February of 1983. Its worldwide membership includes many thousands of members from 64 countries. Among its members are American, German, and Japanese submarine captains from World War Two, top admirals from the United States, the former Soviet Union and Chinese navies as well as scholars and naval enthusiasts from around the world.
The world renowned British Broadcasting Corporation called Shark Hunters the "most respected and authoritative" source in the world on the history and activities of World War II German U-boats.
Shark Hunters membership is open to anyone interested in the fascinating world of submarines. Additional information regarding the monthly magazine or membership can be obtained by contacting:
Shark Hunters International Inc.
PO Box 1539
Hernando, FL 34442
Phone (352) 637-2917
FAX (352) 637-6289

Dedication

To Timothy C. Kutta and all the men who fought on the seas during World War Two.

(Title Page) Long, low, and deadly, a U-boat departs for a long patrol in the Atlantic. Once beyond the friendly cover of German air and naval units, only the conning tower watch and lookouts will be outside the hull.

Introduction

The first real submarines, vessels that had a separate propulsion system for both above and below water, were developed by the French in 1896. These early submarines had limited range and carried few torpedoes. They were designed to attack blockading enemy warships or vessels close to the submarine's home port or their area of operations. Only a few of these early French submarines were built, but since France, a major European power at the time, had them, Britain, Russia, Italy, the United States, and Germany soon followed suit with their own designs.

Germany built her first *Unterseeboote* (underwater boat) the U-1 in 1906. This vessel had the markings of a classic U-boat with a long, slender hull, a conning tower amidship, and a single internal torpedo tube. Unfortunately, it was powered by two 394.5 hp gasoline engines which made it more of a fire trap than an effective weapon. Nevertheless, the stage had been set and Germany, like the other world powers, demonstrated that it too could build a submarine.

During the first ten years of the 20th century, most of the world's major navies had submarines and began a concerted effort to develop and test the strategies and tactics that would make their boats effective. This was easier said than done. The early boats had a short range, limited diving capabilities, and few torpedoes; they were essentially a surface vessel with the capability for short term underwater operations. Still, in exercises conducted prior to the First World War, the submarine demonstrated that it could conduct advanced reconnaissance for fleet units, defend vital naval installations, and become an effective hunter when the opportunity presented itself. Nevertheless, submarines were a new weapon and often viewed by the admirals as little more than an adjunct to the battleships and cruisers that were the main units of the world's battle fleets.

The First World War (1914 - 1918) gave the submarine an opportunity to show its potential. While most of the major navies used their submarines for scouting or reconnaissance, the German *Kaiserliche Marine* (Imperial Navy) decided on a different course. The Naval Command allowed their U-boat commanders greater freedom of action and encouraged them to aggressively use their boats to seek out and destroy the enemy — an initiative often granted to German ground and air commanders as well. There were only 24 U-boats ready for action and, although the number was small, the German submarine fleet racked up an impressive score. During World War I Germany launched 373 submarines which sank an impressive 5708 ships — nearly 25% of the world's cargo fleet tonnage. The sinkings were not restricted to mere cargo ships. On 22 September 1914, U9 sank the British cruisers *Cressy*, *Aboukir*, and *Hogue*. Several other warships, both large and small, were sunk or damaged over the course of the war. The threat of the submarine and the torpedo greatly altered the tactics and, in the case of the Battle of Jutland during the spring of 1916, often affected the aggressiveness of admirals and captains commanding large and powerful surface vessels.

The aggressive spirit of the German submarine fleet was not without its costs. The *Kaiserliche Marine* lost 178 U-boats during the war. Thirty-three percent of the U-boats' officers and men were also lost. The impression they left on the Allies, however, was irrevocable. The German U-boats were specifically mentioned in the Versailles Treaty which ended World War I in November of 1918. Under the terms of the treaty, Germany could not build submarines for the small navy allowed her after the war. It appeared for all intents and purposes that the U-boat was gone forever.

Germany, despite the restrictions of the Versailles Treaty, realized more than any other nation what a valuable offensive weapon the U-boat had become. Shortly after the war the German Navy (renamed *Reichsmarine* in April of 1921) opened a U-boat office in the Mines and Torpedo Inspectorate at Kiel — one of the German Navy's largest naval bases. While the new office could not build any submarines, the officers assigned to the office could monitor submarine construction and technology in other countries and prepare plans for the eventual reinstitution of submarine construction in Germany. The office became a department of the Naval High Command and moved to Berlin.

Eventually, the Germans found a way to circumvent the Versailles Treaty regarding submarine construction. A corporation known as Ingeniueur-Kantoor voor Scheepsbouw (I.v.S), sponsored by Krupp, the German steel and armament giant, was created in the Hague, Holland during 1922. The new company was ostensibly created to design boats

U-1, launched in 1906, was Germany's first 'modern' U-boat. U-1 caused little stir at the time since most of the world's navies were concentrating on battleship construction. Nevertheless, U-1 laid the foundation for the *Kaiserliche Marine's* future U-boat force.

for other nations. Since the company operated in Holland, it did not violate the Versailles Treaty and the Germans could design all the submarines they desired. Since I.v.S.'s parent company Krupp owned the Germania Shipyards at Kiel, there was a free flow of information between the two industrial concerns.

The Versailles Treaty also did not specifically prohibit the design and construction of submarine parts in Germany. The German company Zeiss provided optics, MANN built engines, and Lorenz made radios. Other firms provided a wealth of parts and expertise that would eventually allow Germany to begin building new U-boats. Consequently, when Germany resumed building submarines on her own, all of the vital components, precision equipment, and skilled labor was available from German manufacturers.

The design work at I.v.S. produced the prototypes of the German Navy's 250-ton coastal submarine that would be built as U-1 through U-24. The first design to be completed was sold to Finland in 1931. A larger submarine, a 750-ton boat, was built in Spain under a secret agreement with the Spanish Crown during 1933. The U-boat was sold to Turkey after it was finished in 1934. Many of the features of this boat would soon appear on two of the new German Type I U-boats (U-25 and U-26) built during the next few years.

Of course, once each of the submarines had been built, they had to be tested before they were turned over to the respective owners. In order to test the submarines, members of the German Anti-Submarine School were brought to Holland to crew the boats during the initial sea trials. In order to ensure that all was correct, these crews conducted extensive tests of the boats. By the time the boats were delivered the crews were effective submariners and would form the nucleus of the new submarine force.

In addition to building U-boats and training crews, the I.v.S.'s parent company Krupp had to maintain sufficient repair and replacement parts to service new submarines built by their company in the Hague. Although Germany could not technically build submarines, there were

The power of a U-boat was largely unappreciated until U-9, commanded by Otto Weddingen, torpedoed and sank the British cruisers *Aboukir*, *Cressy*, and *Hogue* — all in less than two hours.

no restrictions on repair parts. Between 1933 and 1935 Krupp stockpiled sufficient parts at the Kiel Navy Yard to repair dozens of submarines — several of which did not yet exist. Additionally, there were sufficient parts to build approximately one dozen complete submarines if necessary. In fact, the Kiel Navy Yard soon constructed special sheds which would allow simultaneous construction of up to six submarines.

By 1935 the new German submarine force had a submarine design bureau, experienced builders, and a nucleus of trained officers and crewmen. All that was needed was to appoint a commander and publicly announce that Germany had once again begun building submarines. The first of the two missing elements was quickly put into place when *Kapitän zur See* Karl Dönitz, an experienced U-Boat captain from the First World War, was appointed to head the German Navy's new U-boat arm.

Admiral Dönitz had served aboard the cruiser *Breslau* and battlecruiser *Goeben* during the early years of World War One and was then sent to submarine school during the summer of 1916. After graduation Dönitz served aboard U-39 under the command of Walter Forstmann, one of Germany's most famous submarine aces. Dönitz accompanied Forstmann on four patrols and, by the time he was given his own boat — UC-25 — Dönitz was an experienced U-boat officer.

Despite Dönitz's experience, he was not very successful with UC-25. After his first kill Dönitz was roughly handled by a depth charge attack and forced to return to port. He was then given command of UB-68. This time his luck ran out. While attacking a heavily guarded merchant convoy on 4 October 1918, Dönitz was forced to surface in full view of the enemy warships escorting the convoy. He and his crew were forced to scuttle UB-68 to keep it from falling into enemy hands. Dönitz and most of his men were captured and spent the remainder of World War One in an Allied prisoner-of-war camp.

After the war Dönitz was asked to stay on in the small, 15,000 man post-war German navy and was assigned to a surface torpedo boat squadron in the Baltic. Since Germany was not allowed to have submarines after the war, torpedo boats were the next best means of allowing the former U-boat captains and crews to maintain their skills in attacking enemy vessels with torpedoes.

During the years between World War I and World War II Dönitz

worked on the skills and tactics that he thought would be needed to successfully engage enemy convoys with torpedoes. He and his flotilla worked on coordinated night torpedo attacks. Gone were the 'lone wolf' tactics of the First World War where the first boat to find the enemy attacked. Under the refined tactics the first U-boat to locate an enemy convoy would stay out of weapons range, but within visual contact until other boats could brought up. Once a 'pack' of U-boats had formed, the group would pick the most opportune moment to attack, overwhelm the defenses, and destroy the enemy ships in the convoy. The new tactics were tested in mock battles in the Baltic Sea — northeast of Germany — and on the wargaming tables of the German Naval Staff. By 1929 Dönitz had worked out and refined the tactics that would become the hallmark of the German submarine force in World War Two. Dönitz was assigned to command the light cruiser *Emden* from 1930 to 1934, but when Germany announced during 1935 that they would once again begin building submarines, Karl Dönitz was chosen to command the first flotilla of the new U-boat force.

One of the stipulations of the 1933 bilateral naval treaty between Britain and Germany — known as the *Anglo-German Naval Treaty* — was a total tonnage limit on both submarine forces. Under the terms of the treaty Germany was not only restricted to building 45% of the number of British submarines, but was also limited to 45% of Britain's total submarine tonnage of 52,700 tons. In order to keep the British from becoming alarmed at the rebirth of the German submarine, the total tonnage of the German U-boat force could not exceed 23,715 tons.

On 16 March 1935, 17 years after the end of WW I, Germany, under the leadership of Adolph Hitler and the Nazi Party, renounced the despised Treaty of Versailles. At this point it was more a matter of form rather than substance. Germany had already been rebuilding her ground, air, and naval forces for several years. The formal renunciation of the Versailles Treaty was simply the public acknowledgment that the former allies could not keep Germany from rearming. Nevertheless, Hitler was an astute political leader. In order to placate the British, Hitler promised to keep the German Navy — now known as the *Kriegsmarine* — at a strength of 35% of the British fleet with the one notable exception that the U-boat fleet would be built to a level of 45% of the British submarine force and could, in the event of special circumstances, be enlarged to 100% of the British force.

This limitation accepted by Hitler and the German government was not as great a hindrance as it appeared. The British had less than 59 submarines and the Germans had none. It would take several years for the Germans to build their allotment of approximately 20 U-boats and until then, the submarine guidelines eased British fears without really imposing any limitations on Hitler's Third Reich.

When the construction limitations were dissolved, Germany brought its U-boat builders back from Holland and occupied the large construction sheds at the Kiel shipyard. The first U-boats built were the 250-ton submarines known as **Type II** U-boats. These boats were rapidly assembled from parts Krupp had stockpiled in the yard over the last few years. These submarines were 136.5 feet long, had a 13 foot beam, and a draft of 12.5 feet. Each U-boat had a crew of 23 officers and men and was armed with a 1-pound gun for anti-aircraft defense and three 21-inch torpedo tubes. The submarines were powered by two 350 hp 4-cycle diesel engines and could attain a speed of 13 knots on the surface. Two battery-powered electric motors gave the submarine a top underwater speed of 7 knots. The pressure hull could sustain a dive to a depth of 50 fathoms (300 feet) and the boat carried sufficient diesel fuel to travel 4000 miles on the surface at a speed of 10 knots. These U-boats were intended for use in the Baltic Sea to keep the Soviet or other navies away from the vital iron ore trade routes between Sweden and Germany. They would also become the backbone of the submarine training command.

A second type of boat — the **Type I** submarine — was also built. This boat was based on a World War One German design and had been updated during the years between World Wars One and Two. Variants of this U-boat had been built for Finland and Spain at I.v.S. This boat, at 750 tons, was larger and could operate as far away as the western Mediterranean.

Thanks to the flow of information between I.v.S. in Holland and the Kiel Navy Yard the Germans were able to launch their first U-boat on 29 June 1935 — a mere three and a half months after Hitler rid

U-15, in consort with other U-boats of the *Kaiserliche Marine*, cruises on the surface during the opening days of WW I. U-15 did not last long, however, it was rammed and sunk in August of 1914.

Germany of the limitations on submarine construction. Additionally, the stockpile of extra parts allowed the U-boat construction program to reach full speed in record time. By the end of June of 1935 — after the first submarine had been launched — the Kiel Navy Yard was able to turn out a new U-boat every eight days.

The Kriegsmarine assembled its submarine commanders while the new U-boats were being built. Karl Dönitz was initially assigned a flotilla of three boats during 1935, but during 1936 was promoted to U-boat force commander and given control of both of Germany's submarine flotillas. Dönitz immediately began to forge an effective weapon of war.

Dönitz, in charge of the U-boat force almost from its inception, was in a position to develop the strategy and tactics of the new force and to influence the performance and characteristics of the types of submarines under construction. His tactics, based on his WW I experience and refined in the Baltic during the 1920s and early 1930s, called for large numbers of U-boats to attack enemy shipping at night. Neither of the current submarines in the inventory — the Type I or Type II — could meet this need. The Type II boats, although excellent in the confined waters of the Baltic, were too small to be sent into the North Atlantic or Mediterranean. The Type I boats had the range and firepower necessary to prowl the oceans around continental Europe, but their 750 ton size was a problem. In practical terms that meant that Nazi Germany could only build thirty-one 750 ton U-boats. The Type I design, although possessing great potential, was passed over in favor of other designs.

To carry out his attack philosophy of using 'packs' of submarines Dönitz needed ocean-going, or 'blue-water' submarines. If the Kriegsmarine stayed with the 750 ton boats Dönitz would be limited by the number of submarines he could build until the treaty between Germany and Britain was abrogated. This of course would be a prelude to war and the German U-boat flotillas would have to be prepared to take on the full might of the British fleet while attempting to hunt down the British merchant marine. When this happened Dönitz wanted as

many U-boats as possible. In practical terms this called for a construction program which emphasized medium sized U-boats. Consequently Dönitz was left with the question of what was the smallest sized U-boat that Germany could build which would still be effective as an ocean-going submarine.

While Dönitz searched for the perfect boat to prove his theory on submarine warfare, there were other naval officers who also had theories on the ideal size of German submarines and the tactics they should employ. Several high ranking German naval officers pushed for the construction of large U-boats capable of long range commerce raiding similar to that done by the surface raiders of World War I. These large boats, ranging and raiding in the far flung corners of the world's oceans, would theoretically sink scores of ships and drive enemy naval forces to despair in their attempts to find and destroy them. These U-boats would have the double impact of both sinking enemy commerce and diverting powerful enemy naval forces away from German waters. Germany would only be able to build a few of these boats, but their great size and striking power would more than compensate for their small numbers — theoretically. This school of thought had several powerful advocates and contracts for four 2000 ton 'Cruiser' submarines were allocated for the Kriegsmarine.

While the debate on the value of the 'U-Cruisers' construction continued, Dönitz and his Chief Engineer, *Kapitän* Otto Thedsen, refined the design of the new medium-sized U-boat. The new boat was designated the **Type VII** U-Boat and had a displacement of 517 tons and a range of 8700 miles. It was powered by two 1400 hp, MANN 6-cylinder, 4-stroke diesel engines which provided a surface speed of 16.5 knots. The new design had an underwater speed of 8 knots using a pair of electric motors and could submerge in as little as 20 seconds. The Type VII U-boat was armed with four torpedo tubes forward and one tube aft and could carry twelve to fourteen torpedoes. The new boats were easy and relatively inexpensive to build and, under the terms of the Anglo-German Naval Treaty would allow the Germans to build 47 submarines. This would give Dönitz the number of U-boats he needed to carry out his 'wolf pack' tactics.

Even during 1933 and 1934, Dönitz was looking to the potential problems of the next war. He had no doubt that he and his submarines would fight either the individual or combined French and British fleets — despite the assurances from Hitler that there would be no war with

A UB Type III U-boat slices through a choppy sea off the German coast sometime during 1917. The UB III boats set the pattern for much of Germany's future U-boat design. Several dozen were built. Admiral Karl Dönitz commanded — and lost — UB-68, a UB Type III boat, during the fall of 1918.

Britain. Dönitz estimated a need for 300 U-boats to successfully engage the naval and merchant marine forces of the enemy. Although this number may appear excessive, it represents a force which would have 33% of its boats on active patrol, 33% in port for refitting, and 33% in training. Consequently, only 100 U-boats would be on active patrol at any one time.

By the end of 1935 the German Naval High Command evaluated their position in view of the current state of world affairs. Among its many observations was that the Type VII U-boat force then under construction did not have the range to reach the western Mediterranean. Since the western Med — and the Straits of Gibraltar — were traditional British and French naval strongholds, the prospects of giving two potential enemies free rein in a vital portion of the world seemed to be a glaring flaw in Germany's strategic planning. In order to correct the problem, the Naval High Command suggested that the Type I boat, which possessed the necessary range, be modified for operations with the current fleet and a portion of Dönitz's U-boat tonnage be allocated to rebuilding the modified Type I boats.

The submarine designers took the basic Type I U-boat and modified it for operations in the Mediterranean and North Atlantic against French or British naval units. The modified design was redesignated the **Type IX** U-boat. It was 244.5 feet long, with a beam of 20.5 feet, and a draft of 13.5 feet. These boats were armed with one 105mm gun, two 20mm anti-aircraft guns, and six 21-inch torpedoes tubes. The engines provided 3200 hp and a surface speed of 18.5 knots, while the electric motors provided eight knots of speed underwater. The Type IX U-boat had a range of 6,500 miles at 12 knots. Eight boats were included in the initial order with the first boat scheduled for completion during the summer of 1938.

By the end of 1935 the U-boat force that would begin the Second World War was already under construction. Twelve Type II boats were completed. The Deutsche Werke in Kiel completed U-1 through U-6 while the Germania firm built U-7 through U-11, U-17, and U-20. Additionally, the first Type VII boats — U-29 through U-31 — were under construction and the first, U-29, would be completed in April of 1936. The great 'U-Cruiser' submarines would stay on the drawing boards for a few more months before their great size and complexity convinced the German Admirals that they should be scrapped. However, until these boats were officially canceled their proposed tonnage was counted toward the German quota of submarine tonnage under the Anglo-German Naval Treaty.

While the various types of U-boats were under construction, Dönitz began to train his crews in earnest. He searched out the best and brightest in the Kriegsmarine to lead them. He valued young, aggressive officers to the older, more staid veterans. He instilled an aura of elitism into the officers and men and drilled them relentlessly in his system of night 'pack' attacks. The officers and men under

With the end of WW I came the end of the *Kaiserliche Marine* and its most important and powerful ships. U-boats were specifically mentioned in the Treaty of Versaille and were forbidden to the remnants of the German Navy. Here, U-boats are broken up for scrapping. A few boats were parcelled out to other nations as part of Germany's war reparations. (GW via Ken McPherson)

training were given 14 attack exercises per week. These included both day and night attacks and were conducted both on the surface and submerged. These attacks incorporated both Dönitz's new tactics and an operational appreciation for the current anti-submarine weapons of potential adversaries. U-Boat captains were taught to patrol on a line in order to sweep a greater area of the sea and improve their chances of detecting enemy targets. Once the enemy was contacted the first boat would radio the position of the ship and shadow the vessel until reinforcements arrived. Only then would the attack begin. This allowed the U-boats to launch a succession of attacks designed to confuse the enemy as to the exact strength and location of the U-boat(s) and to provide such an offensive punch that a U-boat pack might overwhelm the defenses and destroy an entire convoy. Underwater attacks during the day were conducted 3000 yards (1.5 nautical miles) from the target. This was the effective range of *Asdic*, an early version of sonar, and Dönitz fully understood the technology of Asdic and its limitations. Night attacks were taken in closer and all the submarine crews were thoroughly trained on the use of their powerful deck guns.

Even as Dönitz was welding new crews and boats into an effective weapon of war, the German High Command was establishing new priorities. The Naval Z Plan was promulgated during 1937 and established the types and numbers of ships that would be needed in the event of a naval war with Great Britain. The plan called for the creation of a fleet of heavily armed light cruisers which would be used as commerce raiders to destroy the British merchant fleet and tie down valuable elements of the British Navy. In order to get the cruisers through the British naval blockade which was certain to be imposed at the beginning of a new war, the Z Plan also called for the construction of several powerful battleships and two aircraft carriers which would allow the German cruisers to leave and reenter port. The allocation of the naval budget to this massive capital ship construction program robbed the submarine force of valuable funding and raw materials. The U-boat arm suddenly became a secondary force due to the international requirement to stop a merchant ship and allow the crew to disembark before it was sunk by a submarine. The German admirals believed that this international requirement would expose the submarines to attack by aircraft and convoy escorts which, in turn, would greatly limit their effectiveness. Dönitz's wolf pack tactics would only work if Germany practiced 'unrestricted' submarine warfare as she had during World War One. Under the current naval planning, unrestricted submarine warfare was not a consideration. The Naval Staff's revised thinking under the Z Plan relegated the German submarine force to a secondary role and only allowed the U-boat arm to expand to 174 submarines by 1945 — and a full 33% of these would be the smaller Type II coastal boats. It was obvious that Dönitz was not only not going to get the 300 boats he felt he needed to be effective in the next war.

When faced with the Z Plan Dönitz and his submariners were undaunted. They crewed their boats with great élan and continued to train at a relentless pace. During fleet maneuvers in the spring of 1939 four groups of U-boats located and overwhelmed a convoy in a mock attack. The attack substantiated Dönitz's tactics and confirmed the high level of training and readiness of his U-boat crews. This was indeed fortunate, since the 1945 war the admirals had predicted under the Z-Plan would actually begin during the fall of 1939.

(Above) UA, a mine laying U-boat built for the Turkish Navy, was incorporated into the Kriegsmarine. UA was the only boat built of this class. The bridge was extended to form an additional platform for an 88mm gun.

(Below) During the inter-war years of the 1920s and 1930s, German submarine designers maintained their expertise by designing boats for other nations. Saukko, designed and built for the Finnish Navy, was one such boat. The boat was designed for coastal operations, but has a strong resemblance to the later Type VII U-boats of WW II.

The Happy Times, 1939 - 1942

Germany invaded Poland on 1 September 1939 and the Poles were crushed within a matter of weeks. Prudent Polish diplomats, fully aware that Germany might invade, had signed mutual defense treaties with France and England and within a few days both had declared war on Germany. The Second World War had begun in Europe.

The German Kriegsmarine was notified of the impending invasion during August. Dönitz received the news on 15 August and immediately executed his war plans to get his 46 U-boats to sea before the anticipated British blockade trapped them in their bases. Twenty-two of the boats were the ocean going Type VIIs or IXs, while the remaining twenty-four were the smaller Type II coastal boats. Still, Germany was at war and Dönitz intended to use all of the U-boats at his disposal to strike at the enemy. During the next week eleven Type VII boats, assigned to the Second U-boat Flotilla, took up their pre-arranged positions along the most likely routes of merchant and naval shipping approaching or leaving Great Britain from its western ports. Five Type IX boats, U-37 through U-41 and assigned to the 7th U-boat flotilla, were sent to the western approaches off Gibraltar where they could intercept ships entering or leaving the Mediterranean. Fourteen of the Type II boats were sent into the Channel and North Sea to defend the German coast and assume positions to intercept British and French shipping. Finally, several of the serviceable Type II boats were sent to the Baltic to keep an eye on the Russians and protect the vital ore trade between Sweden and Germany. The remainder of the boats, now in various states of repair, would be sent to reinforce the North Sea, Channel, or Baltic Sea patrols when they became available. The deployment involved the total available strength of the U-boat force.

All of the boats were notified by message on 1 September 1939 that the situation between Germany, France, and England was still uncertain and that the U-boat captains should conduct themselves accordingly. Even in the event the U-boat captains had been allowed to attack enemy or neutral shipping on the first day of the war, they were still governed by the international agreement that required them to surface, inform the target ship that they would be sunk, and give the ship's crew time to safely abandon and get clear of the vessel. Then, and only then, could the ship be sunk. It was a civilized law which had been largely negated by the use of modern radios, high speed aircraft, and fast moving convoy escorts. A brief signal from the target ship could often bring reinforcements in a short period of time — perhaps even before the U-boat had time to sink its victim. However, it was the international code at the time and Dönitz obliged all of his U-boat captains to comply with the agreement.

Dönitz, however, had unleashed several young and very aggressive submarine commanders into the open waters of the ocean. On 3 September 1939, barely three hours after the notification of hostilities between Germany and France and Britain, *Leutnant* F. J. Lemp, commanding U-30, sighted the 13,581 ton British auxiliary passenger liner *Athenia* steaming south of Rockall Bank on the northwestern approaches to the British Isles. Lemp apparently thought the ship was an armed auxiliary cruiser and unleashed a torpedo which detonated on the port side of the *Athenia* at 2142 hours. The mortally stricken liner sank a few hours later — the first victim of the U-boat campaign of the Second World War.

The sinking caused an international furor as Lemp had not notified the passenger ship of his intentions. In Lemp's opinion the ship was an armed auxiliary cruiser and needed no warning. The sinking of the *Athenia* remained controversial even after the war. However, the incident was a prime example of how archaic the international laws governing submarine attack had become by 1939. Regardless of international law, however, the warring nations quickly realized that there would be little, if any, notification of impending submarine attack.

Other U-boat sinkings soon followed. Between the beginning of the war and 27 September when U-30 (the last of the initial U-boats deployed at the start of the war) returned to port, the German submarines took a considerable toll of Allied shipping. U-26, commanded by *Korvettenkapitän* (KK) Ewerth, sank three ships totaling 17,414 tons using mines. U-27, commanded by KK Franz, sank two ships totaling 624 tons. U-28, commanded by *Kapitänleutnant* (KL) Kuhnke, sank one 4955 ton ship. U-29, commanded by KK Schuhart, sank three ships totaling 19,405 including the British aircraft carrier *Courageous*. *Leutnant* Lemp sank two ships totaling 9625 tons in addition to the *Athenia*. U-31, commanded by KK Habeksot, sank two ships totaling 8706 tons. U-32, under the command of KK Buchel, sank two ships for a total of 5738 tons and damaged two others. KK von Dresky, commanding U-33, sank three ships totaling 5914 tons. U-34, commanded by KK Rollmann, sank two ships which totaled 11,357 tons and took a third ship as a prize. U-35, commanded by KK Lott, sank four ships totaling 7850 tons and damaged another. U-53, commanded by KK

U-6 is moored at pier side. The narrow hull which made the crew's life so uncomfortable also made the submarine difficult to see on the surface and saved many U-boats from attack.

Heinicke, accounted for two ships of 14,018 tons.

The ships of the 7th Flotilla also scored well during the first days of the war. U-38, commanded by KK Liebe, sank two ships totaling 16,698 tons. U-41, commanded by *Leutnant* Mugler, took two prize ships totaling 2,172 tons, and U-48, under the command of KK Schulze, sank three ships totaling 14,777 tons.

The Type II coastal boats also contributed in the first strikes. U-3, commanded by *Korvettenkapitän* Schepke, sank two ships totaling 2348 tons. U-4, under the command of KK von Klot-Heydenfeldt, sank three ships amounting to 5133 tons. U-6, commanded by KK Weingaertner, sank one ship of 3378 tons. U-7, commanded by KK Heindel, sank three ships of 5892 tons. U-36, commanded by KK Frohlich, sank two ships of 2813 tons. U-14, commanded by KK Wellner, attacked the Polish submarine *Zbik* on 3 September, while U-13, U-15, U-16, and U-17 laid magnetic mines off the British coast to interfere with Channel shipping.

Several boats were dispatched with the specific mission of finding and sinking British naval units as they emerged from their harbors. U-12, U-56, U-58, and U-59 were stationed off the Great Fisher Bank, U-9 and U-19 were positioned off the east coast of Scotland, while U-20 was positioned off Norway to intercept any British naval units which might move in that direction. Although these U-boats did not sink any ships they were in position to counter any sudden moves by the Royal Navy.

By mid-September of 1939 most of the boats had reached the end of their operational endurance. When their torpedoes were expended or their fuel ran low, the boats made their way back to their home bases. U-30, the last submarine from the first wave returned to Wilhelmshaven with one engine out on 27 September. The results had been good. The submarines sank 39 ships using torpedoes and had laid sufficient mines to account for several more. Dönitz estimated that his boats sank over 150,000 tons of enemy shipping during the first month of the war. The only losses suffered by the Germans were U-39 — sunk on 14 September — and U-27 which was lost on 22 September.

The heavy Allied losses suffered at the hands of the U-boats during the first weeks of the war alarmed the British Admiralty. During the years before the war, the Admiralty had convinced themselves that the underwater detection capabilities of the new Asdic, or sonar, would virtually neutralize the capabilities of the submarine. The first attack by the U-boats, however, quickly demonstrated that Asdic, although effective, was only part of a defense against submarines. The Admiralty realized that more measures were needed to counter the submarine and immediately instituted several steps to counter German naval power and to protect its shipping from German U-boat attacks. The British announced a naval blockade of Germany on 3 September which was designed to ruin the German war economy as well as detect and destroy German U-boats as they left or returned to port. The British also asked the United States for assistance. Although America was officially neutral it was already obvious that America would eventually enter the war on the Allied side.

At the behest of the British, the Americans instituted 'Neutrality Patrols' in the Atlantic on 12 September. These patrols were ostensibly designed to guarantee the free passage of neutral shipping, but in effect put US warships in close proximity to German U-boats. A mistaken attack by a U-boat on an American warship would be an act of war which would give the United States a reason to enter the war. Finally, the Admiralty ordered the reinstitution of the convoy system and the first transatlantic convoy left Jamaica on 15 September 1939.

Even as the British Admiralty increased its air and sea patrols searching for German submarines, Dönitz was carefully studying the results of the first series of submarine attacks in order to improve their efficiency and effectiveness. It was obvious that the Type II boats were too small to be effective and that there were not enough Type VII boats. The solution was already at hand as three German ship yards were already turning out more, and improved, versions of the Type VII boats. These new boats, designated the **Types VIIA**, **VIIB**, and **VIIC**, were becoming available in greater numbers with each week and more were under construction.

The new boats featured a greater displacement which allowed more room to carry the equipment and weapons needed to stay at sea for longer periods of time. Deck armament was also increased. The VIIC, which would become the standard U-boat in 1940, had a 760 ton displacement, was equipped with five torpedo tubes — four forward and one aft — and mounted an 88mm gun in addition to two 20mm anti aircraft guns on the deck and conning tower. The Type VIIC U-boat could dive to a depth of 400 feet and carried a crew of 44.

Another problem which had come to light during the first attacks was the failure of German torpedoes to properly detonate. Several ships had escaped destruction when the torpedo exploded prematurely or struck the target's hull without exploding. Submarine captains risked their lives and those of the crews to get close enough to fire a torpedo. If the captain missed the target, that was one thing, but to have the target in his sights and have the torpedo malfunction was inexcusable. Dönitz immediately communicated the problem to the chief of the Torpedo Inspectorate who immediately went to work to solve the problem.

At the beginning of the war the Germans had two submarine torpedoes. The first was the 21-inch diameter G7a torpedo which had been developed in 1926. The Kriegsmarine purchased the Horten naval torpedo patents from Norway in 1933 and the Whitehead Fiume patents from Italy in 1938. The combination of the patents and further German research and development had resulted in a torpedo which could sink a merchant ship on impact. The G7a had a range of 6 kilometers and a speed of 44 knots. However, the speed of the torpedo came at a cost. The G7a was driven by compressed air which left a tell tale wake — or trail — of bubbles back to the firing point. Despite this obvious drawback, however, the torpedo was used with great effect. The other standard German torpedo was the G7e which was a 20 foot long, 21-inch diameter torpedo driven by 52 lead-acid electric cells housed in an 11 foot long compartment. The G7e had a maximum speed of 30 knots and a range of 6 km. The loss of speed versus the G7a was compensated by the fact that the electric motor left no visible trail of bubbles while enroute to its target. When it worked correctly it was extremely effective. The torpedo did require careful attention by the submarine crews who were responsible for keeping the cells fully charged and making

U-9 and U-17, two early Type IIB boats, sit at anchor at Warnemunde. These boats were nicknamed 'Dugouts' or 'Canoes' because of their small size. The Type IIB boat displaced 250 tons, were designed for coastal patrols, and armed with four torpedo tubes forward.

sure the torpedo was in working order before it was fired.

Both the G7a and the G7e torpedoes had a 672-pound warhead which could be activated by either contact fuses or the new magnetic detonator. The contact fuse was activated when the nose of the torpedo hit the enemy ship. The force of the contact activated the fuse and detonated the torpedo's explosive charge. The magnetic detonator was activated by the force of the magnetic field generated by the hull of an enemy vessel. The detonator was activated when it ran into the ship's magnetic field which was strongest directly beneath the ship. The explosion could literally lift a ship out of the water and break its keel.

After some review, the Chief of the Torpedo Inspectorate concluded that the problem was that the torpedo was running approximately six feet (or one full fathom) below the crew's torpedo depth setting. In such circumstances, the torpedo would run underneath the target without striking it. This explanation was not good enough since several U-boat captains reported hearing their torpedo hit the target and still not explode.

Dönitz pursued the issue and the Torpedo Directorate conducted additional tests which deepened the mystery without providing any answers. Even as Dönitz ordered his crews back into the war, he was certain that their torpedoes would not always work properly and estimated that between 30% and 40% of the torpedoes fired would probably fail to explode. In Dönitz's estimation that represented almost 300,000 tons of Allied shipping that would be hit by a U-boat and yet escape to deliver its cargo.

The final problem that Dönitz derived from the first report was that the rules of engagement for sinking Allied ships were hopelessly outdated. At the start of the war, the Germans ordered their submarines to sink only Allied shipping. Neutral shipping or ships which could not be identified had to be stopped and searched. In order to do this the submarine had to surface and board the merchant ship. If the ship was found to be carrying war cargo, the crew had to be given an opportunity to abandon the vessel before it was sunk.

The after action reports noted that merchant ships were quick to use their radios when confronted by a surfaced U-boat. These radio transmissions usually brought a quick enemy reaction which put the U-boat and its crew at great risk. The after action reports generated great concern and brought the validity of the legal international requirement into question. Germany was at war, albeit one of her own making, and the High Command was risking precious U-boats and trained crews to the cumbersome workings of an obsolete law. In October of 1939 orders were issued to immediately sink any merchant ship which attempted to use its radio when confronted by a submarine. Additionally, the U-boats operating in the North and Baltic Seas were allowed to attack without warning. Unrestricted submarine warfare, although not total at this point, was well on its way to becoming a reality.

With the arrival of new boats, efforts to correct the torpedo problems, and easing of the rules of engagement, Dönitz felt confident that the next sortie of his boats would be even more effective than the first (although he was well aware of the fact that the British had reinstituted convoy procedures). One of his U-boats, U-31, discovered and attacked a British convoy in the Bristol Channel on 16 September and the report of the attack quickly reached Dönitz's Headquarters. Dönitz, at this point, was not particularly concerned. He was convinced that U-boats using the wolf pack tactics could destroy a convoy. Dönitz wanted to find an enemy convoy and use his wolf pack tactics to overwhelm and completely destroy it. In order to coordinate the attack Dönitz decided to deploy several U-boats with senior officers on board to the key areas where convoys were likely to be found. These officers would, if a convoy was located, take charge of forming the wolf pack and coordinate the attack.

The submarines were refitted, the crews rested, and in early October, the German U-boats slipped out of their harbors and headed to their patrol areas. The patrol areas were much the same as before. Several

boats headed to the west of England to prowl the sea lanes for convoys or ships moving between England and Canada. Others took up stations in the North Sea, the Baltic, the English Channel, and off the coast of Spain. In addition to these boats, Dönitz also selected one boat, U-47 under Gunther Prien, to penetrate the British fleet anchorage at Scapa Flow and attack any warships he found at anchor. It was a bold move, but one intended to display the power of the U-boat and to force the British fleet to withdraw to bases more distant from the German coast.

Gunther Prien was a brilliant and aggressive submarine commander. He found a small unguarded passage into the anchorage and penetrated into the heart of one of the most heavily guarded fleet anchorages in the world on the night of 13/14 October. Although most of the major units of the British fleet had already left the anchorage, Prien located, torpedoed, and sank the old battleship HMS *Royal Oak*. Amid the chaos of the sinking, Prien and U-47 were able to slip out of the anchorage and return to Germany to a hero's welcome.

While Prien was carrying out his daring one boat attack, the other U-boats had arrived in their respective patrol areas and had started a new round of sinkings. One of the first encounters was the location in the North Atlantic of convoy HG.3 on 10 October. News of the find was quickly radioed to Dönitz's Headquarters and nine other U-boats operating in the area were ordered to form a **wolf pack** and attack. The attack was under the command of *Frigatekapitän* (FK) Werner Hartmann in U-36. He was one of the senior officers that Dönitz had detailed to be a tactical commander in the event a convoy was located.

The 9 U-boats immediately began to converge on the convoy. Three of the boats, however, experienced mechanical difficulties and a fourth, U-40, hit a mine and sank on the way to the rendezvous. The five remaining boats arrived on station and began their attacks. U-37, under FK Hartmann, sank eight ships totaling 35,306 tons. U-45, under the command of KK Gelhaar, claimed two ships of 19,313 tons. U-46, under the command of KK Sohler, sank one 7028 ton ship. U-48, under the command of KK Schultze, sank five vessels totaling 37,153 tons, and U-42, under the command of KK Dau, sank a 4803 ton ship. Although the convoy was not protected by accompanying escorts, several warships from other, nearby convoys converged on the German submarines and sank U-42 and U-45. Despite the loss of two U-boats, the

U-41 and U-39 were larger Type IXA U-boats. The white numbers indicate the photo was probably taken before the war started. The numbers were later painted out to avoid compromising the overall gray camouflage. The early *Funkpeilrahmen* or DF loop is visible on the bridge of U-39.

U-26 was one of two Type IA boats built by Germany. This boat was commanded by KL Klaus Ewerth. The boat was difficult to handle, but despite its unsuitability for operations U-26 was pressed into service early in the war and sank three ships. U-26 was sunk by a British Corvette on 1 July 1940.

U-59 was a Type IIC U-boat. Only eight of these small, short-ranged boats were built before being replaced by the larger Type VIIs.

U-60, a Type IIC boat, meets another submarine at sea. Most of the early boats were painted overall light gray. The gray paint and their small size helped them to blend into the horizon. U-60 is equipped with a 20mm flak weapon.

attack was devastating and the convoy was almost wiped out. Seventeen Allied ships, totalling over 103,000 tons and under the supposed safety of a convoy, were sunk by only five U-boats in a matter of hours.

Other U-boats were also busy. U-12, U-16, U-19, U-23, U-24, U-31, and U-33 laid magnetic mines along the sea lanes surrounding the British Isles. U-16 was lost during the operation, but the mines proved to be well placed — accounting for 27,887 tons of Allied shipping sunk and 13,647 tons of shipping damaged.

Four other U-boats were stationed west of the Orkney Islands (off the northern tip of the British Isles) in search of British warships. U-56, under the command of KK Zahn, sighted several British battleships and fired torpedoes at the HMS *Nelson*. Unfortunately, the torpedoes were duds and the battleship continued on unaware that it had even been attacked. Both U-13 and U-59, which had accompanied U-56, were successful during the cruise. Although they did not sink any British warships the two U-boats sank four merchant ships totaling 6136 tons.

A final group of three submarines — U-25, U-34, and U-53 — operating off Gibraltar sighted several enemy ships. U-25, under FK Schutze, sank one 5874 ton ship and U-34, commanded by KK Rollmann, sank another four ships totaling 16,546 tons.

With most of their torpedoes expended, and fuel oil running low, the second wave of U-boats made their way back to their bases for rearming and refueling. During their second war patrol the submariners had accomplished many notable firsts. One of their number had penetrated the British anchorage at Scapa Flow to sink a battleship and a convoy had been subjected to a wolf pack attack and very nearly obliterated. Several other merchant ships were sunk or damaged and at least one enemy capital ship had escaped disaster only because of faulty torpedoes.

The crews returned home to bands on the quays and joyous receptions. Gunther Prien became a national hero and was soon known as 'The Bull of Scapa Flow'. He, along with the rest of his crew, was awarded the Iron Cross First Class. Later, Adolph Hitler himself decorated Prien with the Knight's Cross for his achievements. Prien's exploits, and those of the other crews, soon brought the U-boat service into the spotlight. The captains and crews soon became the darlings of the Nazi propaganda machine. Dönitz was promoted to Admiral on 1 October and his title was changed from Commander of Submarines to Commander-in-Chief of Submarines.

Despite the successes of the previous month there were still areas of concern. The torpedo problem had not been entirely solved. The wolf pack tactics had proved successful, but only one had actually been able to carry out an attack. Dönitz wanted to form several packs which would roam the sea destroying several convoys in a single patrol. Only by destroying dozens of ships in a month could the German submarines hope to strangle Britain's seaborne life line to the rest of the world. In order to create several packs, however, Dönitz needed more boats and the production of new boats was lagging. The German military now had dozens of priority items to deal with and new submarine production seemed to be steadily dropping on the priority list. New

U-boat production was insufficient to keep up with losses much less increase the size of the submarine fleet.

Even as Dönitz and his staff wrestled with these problems the U-boats were rearmed, refueled, and refitted. The submarines went back to sea in late November. Five boats patrolled off the Orkneys in search of British warships, several boats operated in the English Channel, and thirteen other boats kept watch on the east coast of Britain. The smaller submarines laid mines in the critical sea routes around the British Isles, while the remaining boats searched for merchant shipping. Three additional U-boats kept watch on the western approaches to the British Isles.

Despite the harsh winter weather, dud torpedoes, and the reduced number of boats deployed at sea, the aggressive — and now veteran — U-boat crews gave a good account of themselves. Over 98,401 tons of enemy shipping was torpedoed and sent to the bottom while an additional 22,472 tons of shipping ran afoul of mines laid by German submarines. The only loss to the Germans was U-35 which, on 29 November, was discovered and sunk by British destroyers east of the Shetland Islands. Although the U-boats' score was impressive, none of the submarines encountered a convoy during this patrol and there was no opportunity to form a wolf pack in order to overwhelm and destroy a convoy.

By the end of 1939 German U-boat crews had every reason to be proud. They had taken a small force of submarines out against the British Royal Navy — at the time judged to be the most powerful navy in the world — and had inflicted serious damage on both its warships and merchant fleet. The U-boats had proved that their tactics were sound and that the pre-war perception that Asdic would make submarines obsolete was incorrect. The morale of the men was also high. They, like their commander Karl Dönitz, believed that with more boats and an effective torpedo, the U-boats could isolate the British Isles from their overseas empire and knock them out of the war.

There was another reason for the great optimism in Dönitz's headquarters. The German radio intercept service, *B-Dienst*, had been monitoring Allied naval radio traffic since the start of the war. These radio intercepts often gave the location and direction of individual ships or convoys. Although Germany's ability to read the intercepts was sketchy at first, toward the end of 1939 they were confident enough of their abilities to determine the location of several convoys. This information was sent directly to Submarine Headquarters where Dönitz and his staff were able to create an overall intelligence picture of the location and movement of various Allied convoys. The likely location of targets were then passed on to the U-boats already out on patrol.

At the beginning of 1940 the U-boats once again set out on patrol. U-25, U-44, U-51, and U-55 established their patrol area in the North Atlantic. These boats, commanded by veteran captains, soon began to score. U-25, under the command of FK Schutze sank 27,335 tons of shipping. U-44, under the command of KK Matthes, sank eight ships totaling 30,885 tons. U-51, under the command of KK Knorr, sank two ships of 3,143 tons. U-55, under the command of KK Heidel, sank six ships totaling 15,853 tons of shipping. However, during its last attack, U-55 was located by Allied air and naval forces. The U-boat survived a vicious attack by Allied forces, but had to be scuttled to avoid capture.

Eighteen other U-boats moved into position along Britain's eastern coast in search of Allied ships. Numerous kills were recorded, but several boats reported torpedo misfires. Two other boats, U-31 and U-34,

U-60 was commanded by by KL Georg Schewe. The boat was used to lay mines along enemy shipping lanes which accounted for at least one enemy ship. On 10 September 1940 Schewe was transferred to another boat and U-60 was relegated to second line duties. Schewe would go on to sink 15 other ships and receive the Knight's Cross on 23 May 1941.

U-35 shows the sleek lines of a Type VIIA U-boat. The boat was commanded by KL Werner Lott and scored early successes during September and October of 1939. The boat was engaged by three destroyers east of the Shetland Islands on 29 November 1939. Against such odds, the U-boat had little hope of survival and was sunk.

U-38, a Type IXA boat, returns from patrol displaying a number of victory pennants and a weathered finish. U-38 was commanded by KL Heinrich Liebe and scored its first success on 6 September 1939.

laid mines along the key waterways near Falmouth and Loch Ewe.

U-26, U-37, and U-48 were sent into the North Atlantic to locate a British aircraft carrier task force which had been identified by radio intercepts. Despite the accuracy of the intelligence, however, the German boats were unsuccessful. While the three U-boats searched in vain for the British carrier, six other U-boats headed into the North Atlantic in early February in search of merchant shipping. These boats encountered several enemy merchant ships and, in a few days, sank over 47,000 tons of shipping.

In mid-February of 1940 Dönitz established another U-boat group under the tactical command of FK Hartmann in U-37. Hartmann's group consisted of five other U-boats and their mission was to find and destroy a convoy. Their patrol area was established off the coast of Spain and all of the boats were in position within one week. The area chosen was quite fortunate since German intelligence soon reported two enemy convoys moving into the area and Dönitz's headquarters passed the infor-

mation about the approaching convoys to Hartmann. Hartmann was unable to locate either convoy, but during the search his boats found and sank four merchant vessels sailing independently. Unfortunately, Hartmann's U-boat group suffered heavy losses. Both U-53 and U-54 were located and sunk by British air and surface units which had increased their activity in the area due to the passage of the convoys.

On 18 February the German Navy launched OPERATION NORD-MARK — a sortie by major elements of the German surface fleet into the North Sea. The Germans hoped to disrupt Allied naval traffic moving between Norway and England. Seven U-boats were involved in the operation and they sank thirteen ships including a destroyer.

U-boats continued to prowl the North Sea for the remainder of February. U-63, under the command of *Leutnant* Lorentz, located convoy HN 14, but before he could attack, his U-boat was sunk by Allied escorts. U-14, U-17, and U-20 had better luck. Between 29 February and 9 March 1940 the three U-boats found and sank six merchant ships

Torpedo men load a G7 torpedo aboard U-8. The deck gun has been turned to port to allow the 'eel', as the Germans called their torpedoes, to fit onto the loading ramp. The loading ramp allowed the torpedo to slide below deck where the crew below could stow it. U-8 was a Type IIB U-boat. U-8 wears an overall gray camouflage scheme with a dark gray or green dapple on the conning tower and hull. Such schemes were common as the war progressed. The schemes were designed to make the boat more difficult to see, or once spotted, to confuse an observer's estimation of the boat's course and speed.

totaling 16,456 tons.

In early March, U-28, U-29, and U-32 were sent on a mission to lay mines off several major British ports. The boats laid mines off Portsmouth, Newport, and Liverpool and their placement quickly proved effective — sinking two ships in a matter of days. On their return to port the U-boats sank two additional merchant ships. The score could have been higher had it not been for another round of torpedo failures.

On 5 March Dönitz ordered the submarines to concentrate on British warships — likely in preparation for the upcoming invasion of Norway. A force of nine U-boats was assembled and dispatched to patrol both sides of the Orkney and Shetland Islands. Only one British warship, a battlecruiser, was sighted during the patrol. U-44 tried to get into position to launch an attack on the battlecruiser, but was quickly discovered and sunk by the escorting destroyers. Despite the lack of warship sightings, however, the U-boats sank six merchant ships totaling over 15,000 tons.

During the latter part of March, Dönitz ordered thirteen U-boats to hunt down and destroy British and French submarines operating in the North Sea. It was a difficult task and one not particularly suited to the U-boats. The German submarines did not account for any Allied submarines during the patrol, but did locate and sink six cargo ships totaling over 12,000 tons. Ironically U-22, one of the boats engaged in the hunt for enemy submarines, was rammed and sunk in the Skaggerrak (off the northern tip of Denmark) by an enemy submarine.

In April of 1940, the U-boats concentrated their operations on supporting the invasion of Norway. The submarines patrolled the likely shipping routes between England and Norway in search of both enemy warships and merchant vessels. U-38 fired torpedoes at the British cruiser *Effingham* and Gunther Prien in U-47 fired on the battleship *Warspite*. Luck was with the Allies and faulty torpedoes resulted in no score for the Germans. U-24 also managed to get into position to attack

(Above) U-29, a Type VIIA boat, was commanded by KL Otto Schuhart, and still wears its early pennant number on the conning tower. Schuhart sank a total of 12 ships totaling 83,668 tons, but his most successful attack was the sinking of the British aircraft carrier *Courageous* on 17 September 1940. Schuhart ended the war as the Commander of I Section of the Flensburg-Murwik Naval Academy.

(Below) U-48, a Type VIIB boat, returns to port. The heavily chipped paint indicates a long patrol and the crew is ready and anxious for shore leave. The boat was commanded by KL Herbert Schultze. He was known as 'daddy' to his crew and took good care of them. He was also known for taking care of the survivors of the ships he sank by summoning neutral ships to the area of his sinkings.

the cruiser *York*, but was driven off before it could carry out an attack.

The U-boats continued their screening operations off Norway until the end of April. By the end of the Norwegian campaign most of the boats needed major overhauls or refitting. Additionally, the U-boat arm was finally expanding and more boats were needed in the training flotilla. Many of the boats that had gone to sea during the first months of the war were battered and in need of repair. When the worst boats returned to port many were simply relegated to training command in lieu of an attempt to fix all of the problems that months of heavy combat had caused. Although small numbers of U-boats continued to prowl the North Sea, the boats did not reappear en mass until June. By then, France had succumbed to the German *Blitzkrieg* (lightning war) and the availability of bases on the western coast of France had shortened the outward trip to the Atlantic by 450 miles. Additionally, the Luftwaffe was now able to station long range patrol aircraft, such as the Focke Wulf Fw 200, at coastal bases. These patrol aircraft could range far out to sea searching for, and often attacking, Allied shipping. Contact reports were quickly relayed to U-boats on patrol. The loss of France also forced the British to cover both the northern and southern routes into the Atlantic. The combined effects created an atmosphere very conducive to U-boat operations and this period soon became known as the 'fat' or 'happy time'. In June the U-boats sank 58 ships, amounting to 284,000 tons and in July an additional 38 ships — amounting to 196,000 tons — were sent to the bottom.

The lack of, or at least thinly spread, British anti-submarine warfare ships, coupled with the ability to get into the Atlantic shipping lanes rapidly and without being detected, quickly raised the morale of the U-boat crews. New Type VII boats also began to arrive from the U-boat construction yards. The torpedo issue was also solved when the Torpedo Directorate issued orders to use only the reliable contact fuses and abandon the use of the magnetic exploders. Finally, on 17 August, Hitler gave the submarines free reign when he announced a total blockade of

the British Isles and ordered any ship found in those waters sunk.

Karl Dönitz was still unhappy. Despite the successes of June and July, most of the Allied ships which had been sunk were not in a convoy, but rather sailing independently. These merchant vessels were easy targets for individual U-boats. Dönitz had not had an opportunity to prove his wolf pack tactics, nor could he readily determine if his command and control theory of placing a senior commander in tactical command would work. In late August all the pieces came together for Dönitz to test his theory.

On 30 August 1940 German intelligence detected the location of convoy SC-2. All U-boats in the area were immediately directed to intercept the convoy. Four U-boats found the convoy and, over the next few days, sank five ships totaling 20,943 tons. The attack ended when the Allies sent air and surface units to protect the convoy. The U-boats broke off the attack, but the four remained in the area to continue their patrol. On 20 September convoy HX-79, passing through the same area, was discovered by U-47 which notified Dönitz's Headquarters. A new wolf pack was quickly assembled by sending six new boats to join the four already on station. Once the pack was formed the attack began. During a running battle over the course of several days the German U-boats sank 12 of the 41 ships in HX-79. The lost vessels amounted to 77,863 tons of Allied shipping. The U-boats also sank one escort from Convoy SC-3 which came to the aid of the beleaguered HX-79.

The heavy loss of ships in an escorted convoy was a heavy blow to the Allied anti-submarine strategy. The loss of the 12 ships in the convoy added to the others sunk during the month brought the total Allied losses for August to 59 ships amounting to 268,000 tons of shipping. The figures were staggering. Dönitz's wolf pack theory had been validated. The German Admiral had discovered a way to defeat the Allied convoy system. In fact, he had discovered a way to defeat the Allies. If Dönitz's U-boats could sink more shipping and supplies than the Allies could replace, he could force the British to surrender without the need for an invasion. The overall plan became known as the 'tonnage war'. All the Germans needed were more U-boats and a bit of luck.

The wolf packs continued their successes into October of 1940 when bad weather began to limit operations in the Atlantic. In October 63 ships of 352,000 tons were sent to the bottom for the loss of only six U-boats. By November, however, the overworked U-boat force was in

U-102's officers and men, wearing dress uniforms, pose for a picture on the midships deck and the aft conning tower section. The boat was commanded by KL Harro v. Klot-Heydenfeldt. U-102 left Lorient, France on its last patrol on June 17, 1940. The boat sank two ships on 1 July, but was later located and sunk by an Allied destroyer.

16

need of rest and refitting. The heady days of summer were replaced with the cold storms of winter. Even though the majority of the U-boats were brought back into port for repairs, the submariners still managed to sink 32 ships amounting to 147,000 tons of shipping in November and a further 213,000 tons of shipping in December.

By the end of 1940 it appeared that Dönitz's submarine force was on the verge of crippling the Allied war effort. The loss, on average, of a quarter million tons of shipping were far too much for the Allies to replace. If the losses continued unabated, England would soon be brought to its knees. The Allies' reaction to the U-boat threat had been spotty at best. The lack of submarine chasers could only be rectified by building new and better ships. New ship construction programs took time, however, and until they were built the, best the British Admiralty could do was swap fifty old World War I destroyers from the United States in return for US basing rights in British possessions overseas. The Allies gradually reinforced the concept of the convoy system, although they allowed ships to travel by themselves as late as October of 1940. The heavy shipping losses convinced the Admiralty that all ships needed to be in a convoy and the system was tightened to insure safety. The most effective antisubmarine weapon was the aircraft and, although there were not many long range patrol aircraft available, those that were became increasingly involved in antisubmarine patrols.

German successes in September and October of 1940 finally awakened the Allies to the seriousness of the U-boat threat. As a result the haphazard nature of Allied antisubmarine defenses became more systematic. In September, the United States agreed to take over convoy protection in the Western Atlantic. This allowed the British to concentrate their efforts on convoys in the Eastern Atlantic and virtually doubled the number of escorts available for that vital duty. The Royal Navy was also able to provide more destroyers and escorts as the threat of a German invasion of the British Isles dissipated during the fall of 1940. British Coastal Command was brought under the operational control of the Admiralty on 4 December 1940. This allowed the British Navy to direct the aircraft of Coastal Command to escort the most critical convoys as they left or approached the British Isles.

British intelligence also went to work to decipher the German naval codes. If the Royal Navy could break the code they would be able to determine the location of each U-boat when it radioed in its position

each day. The scientific community was also hard at work developing new ways to locate the U-boats at sea. In January of 1941 a new, smaller radar set was developed which could be used on aircraft as well as ships. The new radar sets allowed ships and aircraft to locate U-boats running on the surface — often beyond visual range. Radio signal locating devices such as the High Frequency Direction Finder (HF/DF or Huff Duff) were also developed. These sets could be used to locate the U-boats when they surfaced to transmit their daily coded signal reports back to U-boat Headquarters. Even if the code could not be broken the electronic locating system would allow the Royal Navy to determine the location of a U-boat to within a 25 mile radius and attack or avoid the submarines as appropriate.

The British also centralized all of their intelligence information regarding U-boats into the Submarine Tracking Room of the Admiralty's Operational Intelligence Section. The Admiralty tracked every positive contact — and best guess — on the location of U-boats at sea. By the winter of 1940 the men and women of the Submarine Tracking Room were quite adept at determining the location of deployed U-boats and routing Allied convoys around them.

The growing Allied response was still some months away from reaching its full potency, however, and until all of the various facets of the antisubmarine defense came on line and integrated into an effective defense, the U-boats would continue to present a potent threat. The threat would be the greatest in the area known as the 'Atlantic Gap'.

The Atlantic Gap was a 300 mile wide gap in the mid-Atlantic that was outside the range of most Allied patrol aircraft — whether operating from the British Isles or the United States. The Germans realized this weakness in the Allied defenses and this Gap became a favorite hunting ground for U-boats. The Allies already had several types of very long range patrol aircraft such as the Consolidated B-24 Liberator bomber or Short Sunderland flying boats which had the range to narrow the gap. However, these long range aircraft were in short supply and it

The officers and crew of U-79 stand in formation on the afterdeck. U-79 was commanded by KL Wolfgang Kaufmann and operated in the North Atlantic and Mediterranean where it sank several enemy ships.

(Above) KL Adalbert Schnee, the commander of U-60, reclines next to his score of 41,000 tons of enemy shipping sunk. Schnee, commanding a Type XXI boat, had a British cruiser in his sights when the war ended in May of 1945. He called off the attack, returned to base, and surrendered.

(Below) U-141, a Type IID boat, enters a French port wearing alternating vertical bands of light and dark gray camouflage paint. The scheme was designed to break-up the U-boat's outline and make it more difficult to see against the horizon.

(Above) The jubilant crew of U-52, a Type VIIB boat, returns from patrol. The boat was commanded by KL Wolfgang Barten at the beginning of the war and then taken over by KL Otto Salman. The deck was widened around the gun to provide greater operating space for the gun crew.

(Above) The crew of a Type VII boat lounges on deck while the boat moves through a crowded harbor. Entering and leaving harbor was one of the few times a crew was able to relax on deck.

(Below) U-124, a Type IXB boat, passes a German surface ship. Even at close range the low silhouette makes the boat difficult to see. U-124 was commanded by KL Georg Wilhelm Schulz. He sank 19 ships totaling 89,986 tons. Schulz was awarded the Knight's Cross and ended the war commanding the 25th U-boat Flotilla at Travemünde.

(Above) U-126, a Type IXC boat, returns from patrol in company with the Type VIIA U-boat U-31. U-126 was commanded by KL Bauer. He graduated from the Naval Academy in 1933 and was nicknamed 'dwarf' due to his small size. Bauer ended the war in command of the 26th Training Flotilla at Pillau.

would be several months before they would be made available in the necessary quantity for antisubmarine operations. The best the Allies could do until then was to coordinate their current antisubmarine air efforts until more aircraft became available.

While the Allies prepared their convoy defenses for the new year, the Germans resumed their own operations. Dönitz realized that his U-boats were on the verge of a great victory although he needed more boats to ensure success. In January of 1941 the U-boat construction yards turned out eleven new U-boats bringing the total number of operational boats to 120. While U-boat production was increasing, there were still too few boats for Dönitz's liking. In order to put more boats at sea he ordered the quickest possible turn around of the boats in port in order to maximize the number of boats at sea at any one time. While this did increase the number of boats at sea, it also placed a tremendous burden on the U-boat crews. Dönitz, however, felt the risk was worth the potential rewards and he soon had two or three groups of up to ten submarines each patrolling the northern routes of the Atlantic Ocean.

Despite the ever increasing number of U-boats, their captains were finding it difficult to converge en masse on the convoys. The stormy weather in the Atlantic, coupled with the ability of the Allies to determine where the U-boats were patrolling allowed the Allies to route many convoys around the wolf packs. Still the U-boats sank 21 ships totaling 127,000 tons in January and thirty-nine ships totaling 197,000

the following month. Most of these ships were convoy stragglers or running independently.

Dönitz launched his 'Spring Offensive' at the end of February of 1941. He shifted operations to the north, in hope of finding the Allied convoys trying to take advantage of the rough seas of the North Atlantic. He ordered all boats at his disposal to take part in the Spring Offensive. These boats, manned by experienced crews and captains, were capable of causing great destruction to the Allied merchant marine force and perhaps signal the beginning of the end of England's resistance.

The Spring Offensive met with bad luck. The combination of improved Allied antisubmarine techniques and increased use of convoys brought the U-boat skippers up against convoys with heavy and aggressive escorts. Germany lost three of her top U-boat aces in rapid succession. Gunther Prien in U-47 was lost on 8 March 1941. On 17 March *Kapitänleutnant* (KL) Joachim Schepke was rammed and sunk and KK Otto Kretschmer, Germany's leading ace, was captured. Their loss was a great personal blow to Admiral Dönitz who was very close to his U-boat captains. Despite the losses, however, Dönitz was more convinced that the only way to attack heavily escorted convoys was by the use of the wolf pack. Even with the loss of three of his top aces and several other boats, the German submarines were hitting the Allies hard.

More U-boats would be ordered into the Atlantic for the next round of

(Above) U-616 rests in placid waters in this wartime painting. The U-boat arm created a mystique all its own during the war. The service was composed of daring young men who went to sea in small boats to battle the might of the British Royal Navy. Paintings such as this were often printed on post cards.

(Below) U-201 passes another (unidentified) U-boat at sea on 17 June 1941. Clouds of diesel smoke drift between the two boats.

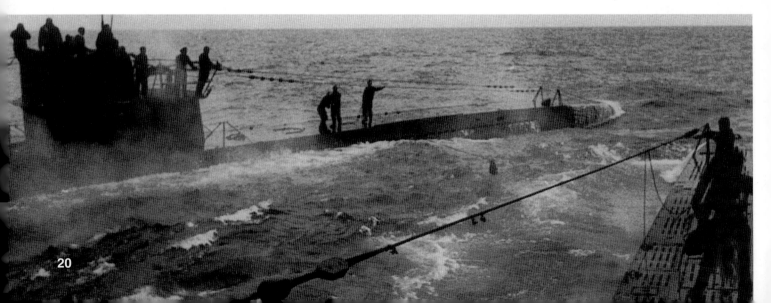

attacks — enough boats to overwhelm the escorts and destroy the convoys. Dönitz did not get far in his efforts thanks to the worsening Italian situation in North Africa. Dönitz was ordered to transfer 20 boats from the Atlantic to the Mediterranean. The Germans had to shore up the Italian position in North Africa and U-boats were required both to stop the flow of Allied supplies to British bases in Cyrenica and Egypt and to keep Allied warships out of the sea lanes used to reinforce Erwin Rommel's growing Afrika Korps.

The diversion of so many U-boats from the North Atlantic effectively ended any massed U-boat attack against an Allied convoy. The German invasion of Russia (OPERATION BARBAROSSA) in June of 1941 drew off additional U-boats. Six U-boats were reassigned in June to patrol the northern waters of Murmansk and Archangel — both vital Soviet ports. These and other commitments continued to sap Dönitz's campaign against the British convoys in the North Atlantic. At one point during 1941, only four boats were in the Atlantic to engage the Allied convoys and their escorts.

British Intelligence scored several victories during the year. They realized that the Germans were using unarmed ships to send coded weather reports back to Berlin. The information was used by the U-boat crews and the *Luftwaffe* to determine when a particular operation might be feasible. The British correctly guessed that these ships could be easily located and captured. The operations against the weather ships began on 28 May and, in a 17 day period, the British captured ten German weather ships. Once captured the weather ships revealed a wealth of information including codes, code ciphers, and other important intelligence data. The British antisubmarine forces also captured U-110 complete with its code books and ciphers. This information, coupled with the information gathered from the captured weather ships, gave British intelligence a clear and comprehensive view of German submarine operations for approximately a three month period.

Despite the setbacks encountered during 1941, the U-boats continued to perform well. In May the boats accounted for 58 ships totaling 325,000 tons. In June the U-boats sank 61 ships with a total loss of 310,000 tons. Sinkings during the months of July and August dropped off with 22 and 23 ships sunk respectively. The number of sinkings continued to be low for the remaining months of the year. In December of 1941 the full weight of the diversity and the intensity of U-boat operations showed on the available boats. Dönitz could only put 12 boats off Gibraltar and 15 in the rest of the Atlantic. The small number of boats accounted for a mere nine ships sunk during the month. By the end of the year, the German U-boat fleet had destroyed 2.1 million tons of Allied shipping.

The entry of the United States into the war in December of 1941 influenced both sides of the U-boat war. While the official declaration of war offered the Allied side the full weight of American military and industri-

(Above) U-74, commanded by KK Eitel-Friedrich Kentrat, leaves port for another patrol. Kentrat commissioned U-74 on 31 October 1940 and sank his first ship in April of 1941. U-74 was one of the few boats which picked up survivors of the battleship *Bismark*. Kentrat ended the war with eight ships totaling 43,301 tons sunk and was awarded the Knight's Cross.

(Below) U-209 is launched at Kiel on 28 August 1941. The boat was commanded by KL Heinrich Brodda who scored several successes in the Arctic during the later summer of 1942.

(Above) U-108 returns to Lorient, France on Christmas Day 1941. KK Klaus Scholtz commissioned U-108 on 22 October 1940 and scored two victories on his first patrol. He had a string of success until he took command of the 12th *U-Flotille* (U-Boat Flotilla) in Bordeaux in October of 1942. He and his staff were captured by the Allies on 11 September 1944.

(Above) U-158, a Type IXC U-boat under the command of KL Erwin Rostin, prepares to move out of port. He commissioned the boat on 25 September 1941 and had a series of successful sinkings in the North Atlantic and off Bermuda. The submarine was sunk by US aircraft near Bermuda on 30 June 1942. Rostin was killed in the attack. At the time of the attack Rostin had sunk 17 ships amounting to 99,170 tons.

(Below) U-124 returns to port after a long cruise. The morale of the U-boats crews was kept high by the warm receptions they received when they returned from patrol. The staff of the Flotillas, and indeed U-boat Headquarters itself, made it a point to greet each boat as it returned. U-124 was a Type IXB boat.

al power, it also opened the entire Western Atlantic and the coast of the United States to the wrath of Dönitz's U-boats.

Dönitz had received many reports from his U-boat captains about the poor state of the defenses along the eastern coast of the United States and the Gulf of Mexico. When the United States entered the war, Dönitz decided to take full advantage of the weakness. He ordered OPERATION ROLL OF THE DRUMS — a U-boat offensive against American coastal shipping — to begin in January of 1942. Out of 91 U-boats at Dönitz's disposal, twenty-three boats were in the Mediterranean and could not be withdrawn. Six were on patrol off Gibraltar and four were positioned off Norway. Of the 58 remaining boats, 25 were in the dock yards for maintenance and half of the remaining 33 boats were either on their way to or returning from their patrol areas.

Still Dönitz wanted to strike the Americans while they were unprepared. Five long range Type IX U-boats had been dispatched to the US between 16 and 25 December 1941. When they arrived off the east coast, the crews found the buildings along the American shoreline still brightly illuminated at night and merchant ships moving independently along the shipping lanes. The ships were silhouetted against the lights on shore and offered the U-boats perfect targets. The German U-boat arm began a second 'happy time' of easy kills. The five U-boats sank 17 ships amounting to 134,000 tons of shipping on their first patrol. These losses, added to the later U-boat kills in January, brought the monthly total to 62 vessels totaling 327,000 tons of shipping sunk.

Admiral Dönitz knew that five boats were not enough to destroy all of the shipping along the American coast. However, his attempts to send more boats were thwarted by the High Command. He requested permission to redeploy the six long range Type IXC boats stationed off Gibraltar to American waters, but the request was refused. Even so, Dönitz ordered all available U-boats to move to the East Coast of the United States. Even as this order was received, Hitler came to the (erroneous) conclusion that the Allies would soon invade Norway and ordered Dönitz to redeploy his boats in the northern waters to counter the Allied threat. Hitler's order reduced the number of U-boats that could be sent across the Atlantic to a mere five — and these merely served to replace those which had started the campaign.

Unable to send more than a handful of U-boats to the theater, Dönitz ordered the construction of resupply submarines. These U-boats, stripped of all but the barest defensive armament could carry extra fuel, torpedoes, and provisions from Germany to the boats operating off the American coast. These boats were nicknamed *Milchkuh* (Milk Cow) by the men and could transfer up to 600 tons of fuel to thirsty U-boats. The first of these boats (U-459) had been launched in April of 1941 — perhaps in recognition of their future need.

After four months of enormous losses at the hands of the U-boats the Americans realized the threat that even a handful of U-boats presented and instituted the convoy system along the American east coast, the Caribbean Sea, and into the South Atlantic. Antisubmarine air and surface patrols were increased and British experts were brought to the United States to give American sailors the benefit of their years of experience battling the U-boats.

By the end of April of 1942 the U-boats were finding fewer and fewer lone targets along the US coasts. Operations were moved into the Caribbean where the full effect of Allied antisubmarine efforts had not yet been implemented. During May and June, 37 U-boats operated in the area and sank 148 ships totaling 752,000 tons. The sharp increase in U-boat attacks brought the full weight of Allied counter measures into the Caribbean and by the end of June the number of sinkings decreased.

Although the number of sinkings had fallen, Dönitz had reason to be satisfied with his efforts. During the first six months of 1942 the U-boats sank 585 Allied vessels totaling 3,081,000 tons of shipping. Twenty-one German U-boats had been lost to the Allied antisubmarine forces, but the construction yards were now making good the losses. By the end of June of 1942, Karl Dönitz had 140 U-boats available for operations.

Even though Dönitz had every reason to be happy with the success of U-boat operations during the first six months of 1942, he realized that the 'happy time' along the American coast was over. The growing concentration of Allied antisubmarine resources in the area would soon have a telling effect. It was obvious to Dönitz that sending his U-boats to the limit of their operational range into an area that was heavily protected by the enemy would only result in heavy losses to his U-boats and crews. If the Allies chose to concentrate all of their defenses along the American coast, then other sea areas had to be vulnerable. He decided to redeploy his boats into the Atlantic and attack the convoys moving from Canada to England. While the U-boats finished their campaign in American waters and headed back into the depths of the Atlantic, a new campaign was brewing.

The Soviet Union was on the verge of collapse in 1942. The Russians needed supplies, tanks, aircraft, and ammunition to sustain their war effort until their factories could be brought back to full war production. Stalin, responding to the relentless advance of the Germans during 1941 and the threat of German air power to his factories, had directed that the bulk of the Soviet factories be moved en masse to new complexes behind the Ural mountains. In order to assist, the Allies sent a series of heavily laden convoys from Britain and the United States to the Soviet port of Murmansk. The Allies used the bad weather of the Arctic fall and winter to open a lifeline to the Soviet Union. It did not take long for Dönitz to realize the implications of

(Above) U-79 rolls in heavy seas during a storm in the Mediterranean in 1941. Unless there was a dire need to recharge the boat's batteries, it was easier to simply ride out the storm submerged.

(Above) The crew of U-116, a Type IXB boat, pulls a refueling hose on board and drags it below decks. Such operations were extremely difficult when the deck crew had to haul heavy hoses across a slippery deck. The operation could only be accomplished in relatively calm seas.

(Below) U-116 refuels U-406 at sea. Such refueling could extend the patrol radius of the submarines by several hundred miles or keep them on station, near enemy sea lanes, for several extra days.

such a lifeline and the U-boat forces stationed in Norway were reinforced. German submarines were sent into Arctic waters to find and destroy the Allied convoys. The first sinking occurred against convoy PQ-13 in March of 1942 when five out of twenty ships were sunk and their precious cargoes lost. The operations intensified throughout the summer and culminated in the epic battle — or slaughter — of convoy PQ-17.

Convoy PQ-17 sailed from Reykjavik, Iceland with 36 ships. The first losses — to German aircraft based in Norway — occurred on 4 July 1942. Believing that a major sortie against the convoy by heavy German surface units was about to occur, the British Admiralty ordered the ships of PQ-17 to scatter and withdrew the escorts. The merchant ships, alone and unescorted, ran into the U-boats on 5 July. During a running battle that lasted several days, the U-boats sank ten ships while Luftwaffe anti-shipping aircraft claimed a further 13. This was the single most successful attack against the Arctic convoys — so successful in fact, that the Germans canceled their surface ship attack. The battle gave the Allies a frightening look at what a combined, and highly coordinated, air/submarine campaign could do — even to a well protected convoy. The campaign in the Arctic waters would continue for several more months, but the Soviet successes on land and her increased industrial production in the new factories behind the Urals alleviated the need for further convoys.

Dönitz now had 331 U-boats in commission. The increase in boats, however, had come with an increase in requirements. German submarine commitments now extended from the Far East to the Arctic. Many of his top U-boat aces and most experienced crews were dead or had been captured. The newer U-boats were technologically better, but in many cases, they were crewed by inexperienced men who were sent into battle against an enemy growing more experienced and deadly with each passing day. As if to underline the problems, two U-boat wolf pack attacks against Atlantic convoys in July had failed miserably.

Still, there were successes. U-593 located Convoy SC-94 in early August and broadcast the alert. Other submarines in the area headed toward the location forming a wolf pack on 6 August. The massed submarines descended on the merchantmen and their escorts and during the next three days the Germans sank 11 Allied ships totaling 52,000 tons. The only German loss was U-210 — sunk by Allied escort ships.

Another convoy, SL-119, was soon located and attacked on August 14. Five merchant ships with a combined displacement of 42,000 tons were sunk. One U-boat, U-556, was badly damaged by the escorts and limped back to port.

The convoy versus wolf pack battles continued throughout the summer and into the fall with much the same result. The U-boats, once a convoy was detected, would mass on the ships and escorts sinking ten or twelve vessels, while losing one or two of their own number.

During the last six months of 1942, the U-boats continued their deadly work. In July, 96 Allied ships totaling 476,065 tons were sunk by the Germans. One hundred and eight Allied ships totaling 544,410 tons were sunk by German submarines in August. In September the U-boats sank 98 additional Allied ships of 485, 413 tons. In October, 94 ships amounting to 619, 417 tons fell victim to the roving U-boats. U-boats sank 109 ships totaling 728,160 tons in November and, in the final month of the year, the Germans claimed 66 ships amounting to 330, 816 tons.

The successes were not without cost. During the year a total of 87 U-boats had been sunk. By the end of 1942 Dönitz had 393 U-boats in commission of which 212 were fully operational boats that could carry the war to the Allies.

While the U-boats continued their deadly work, the Allies were implementing many of their new antisubmarine systems. While some efforts were directed at providing the air and sea escorts with a better opportunity to locate and destroy submarines approaching the convoys, many other efforts were directed at destroying the submarines while they were in port or as they moved into or out of harbor.

Allied heavy bombers pounded the U-boat bases throughout the sum-

The officers and crew of U-99, a Type VIIB boat, pose in their dress uniforms. The crew normally had little opportunity to wear these uniforms — opting instead for more utilitarian clothing while at sea.

1.U-Flotille

2. U-Flotille

3. U-Flotille

6. U-Flotille

7. U-Flotille

8. U-Flotille

9 U-Flotille

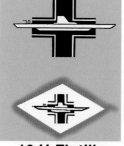
10 U-Flotille

U-3

U-9

U-17

U-26

U-30

U-44

U-101

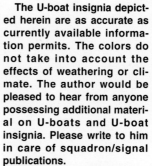

The U-boat insignia depicted herein are as accurate as currently available information permits. The colors do not take into account the effects of weathering or climate. The author would be pleased to hear from anyone possessing additional material on U-boats and U-boat insignia. Please write to him in care of squadron/signal publications.

U-137

U-143

U-149

U-161

U-163

U-164

U-165

U-169

U-175

U-180

U-241

A crewman of U-79 prepares to leave the boat. He is wearing the light blue gray crewman's battle dress.

mer even though, by the time the aerial attacks started, the submarines were safely housed inside massive concrete submarine pens. These reinforced concrete pens proved to be impervious to any weapon except for a direct hit by the largest of Allied bombs. Although the bombing did little actual damage to the pens and the U-boats housed within them, it did disrupt port facilities, slowed the delivery of supplies and equipment, and generally made life miserable for the support personnel working around the yards.

Other Allied technical advances were also proving their worth. Airborne radar proved to be very accurate, detecting surfaced submarines long before the actual aircraft was in view of the U-boat's lookouts. This proved particularly valuable when the Allies began armed antisubmarine patrols over the Bay of Biscay. The Bay was the traditional route the U-boats took when leaving or entering their ports on the western coast of France. Close to home, the boats usually rode on the surface to make better time and were generally not expecting to be attacked. That changed when several U-boats, including U-502 and U-165, were attacked and sunk without warning. Three other boats, U-578, U-705, and U-751 were also badly damaged by aerial attacks while moving across the bay.

The Germans decided to transit the area only at night, but soon found that darkness provided little additional safety. The Allies had provided many of the radar equipped aircraft with a powerful searchlight, known as a Leigh Light, which could illuminate a U-boat from a range of up to a mile. The radar located the U-boat and the light illuminated the submarine so it could be attacked. The combination was deadly.

After losing several boats, the Germans finally realized that the Allies were using a new form of airborne search radar to detect the surfaced submarines. In an effort to counter the Allied radar the Germans began installing French Metox radar detectors on their U-boats. The sets were mounted in the submarines and a length of wire was twisted around a plain wooden cross mounted on the U-boat's bridge. The crews nicknamed this apparatus the 'Biscay Cross', but despite its primitive appearance it did prove effective. U-boats equipped with the Metox detectors could pick up the faint signals of an active search radar several miles before the Allied radar could effectively identify the U-boat. The Germans also began work on developing an air and surface search radar of their own to mount on the U-boats.

The Germans made several other improvements. Antiaircraft defenses on the U-boats were upgraded. Initially, four

7.92mm machine guns were added around the bridge. These were followed by the addition of a single 20mm automatic cannon, and then a quadruple 20mm gun mount. The Germans also added two new torpedoes to the inventory — the *Flachenabsuchender* Torpedo (FAT) and the *Lagenuabhangiger* Torpedo (LUT). Both new weapons had a longer range and more striking power than the earlier G7 series torpedoes.

With all of the new developments on both sides of the battle line it was obvious that 1943 would be the year of decision in the submarine campaign. During the first two weeks of January, patrolling U-boats did not sight or sink an enemy ship due to a series of storms in the North Atlantic. When the weather broke during the last two weeks of January, Dönitz had 164 U-boats ready for action.

(Above) U-751, a Type VIIC boat, commanded by KL Gerhard Bigalk, prepares to get under-way. In December of 1941, Bigalk sank the British aircraft carrier Audacity — the first British escort carrier. U-751 and its crew were lost northwest of Cape Ortegal on 17 July 1942. The word *Antje* painted on the conning tower was a reference to Bigalk's young daughter.

(Below) The conning tower of U-376, a Type VIIC boat, is covered with ice during a patrol in March of 1942. U-376 was commanded by KL Friedrich-Karl Marks. He sank one ship and had two probables during patrols which covered March, April, and July of 1942.

U-88, a Type VIIC boat, submerges in a German port on 4 April 1942. These dives may not have been necessary in port, but such practice shaved precious seconds off dives under battle conditions — often the difference between life and death.

U-9 was an early Type IIB U-boat. These boats were generally painted light gray before the war. U-9 was commanded by FK Wolfgang Luth who scored a number of kills in February and May of 1940.

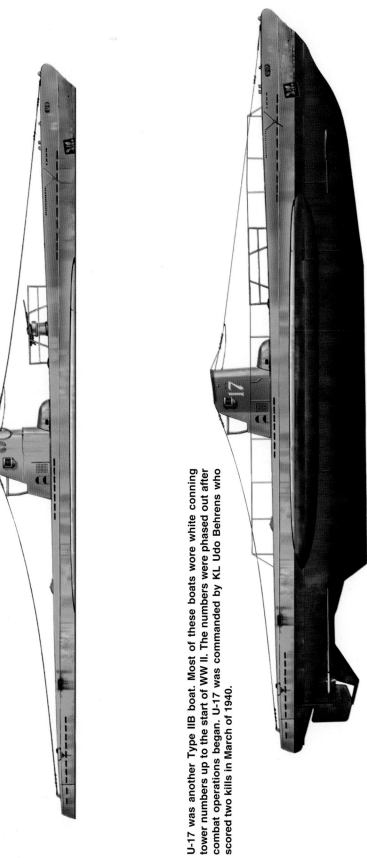

U-17 was another Type IIB boat. Most of these boats wore white conning tower numbers up to the start of WW II. The numbers were phased out after combat operations began. U-17 was commanded by KL Udo Behrens who scored two kills in March of 1940.

U-26, a Type IA boat, wore a camouflage of light gray with a white conning tower number. U-26 scored three kills early in the war, but was herself sunk by a British Corvette on 1 July 1940.

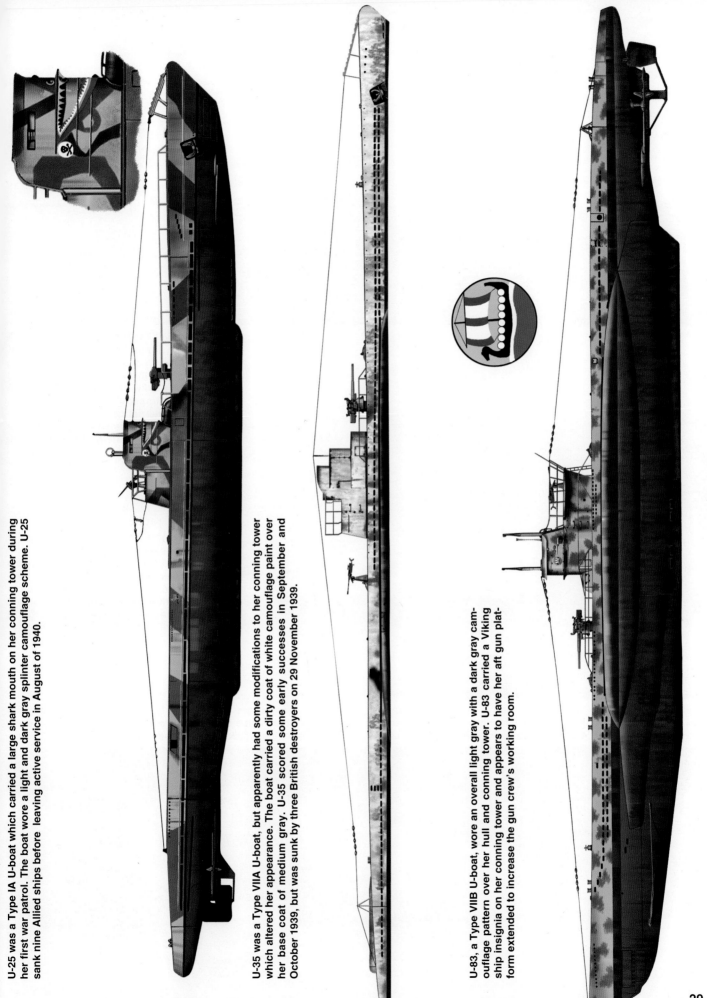

U-25 was a Type IA U-boat which carried a large shark mouth on her conning tower during her first war patrol. The boat wore a light and dark gray splinter camouflage scheme. U-25 sank nine Allied ships before leaving active service in August of 1940.

U-35 was a Type VIIA U-boat, but apparently had some modifications to her conning tower which altered her appearance. The boat carried a dirty coat of white camouflage paint over her base coat of medium gray. U-35 scored some early successes in September and October 1939, but was sunk by three British destroyers on 29 November 1939.

U-83, a Type VIIB U-boat, wore an overall light gray with a dark gray camouflage pattern over her hull and conning tower. U-83 carried a Viking ship insignia on her conning tower and appears to have her aft gun platform extended to increase the gun crew's working room.

(Above) The crew of U-40, a Type IXA boat, loads an 'eel'. The torpedo, minus its fuse is hoisted from the dock to the waiting crew. Loading was a slow and careful process due to the torpedo's weight and its delicate internal components. The conning tower has an unusual splinter camouflage pattern of light and dark gray.

(Left) U-376 pulls along side a Norwegian fishing boat, probably in search of fresh food for the crew's dinner. Such occurrences only happened in friendly waters and it is not known if the transfer was voluntary on the part of the Norwegians. U-376 was a Type VIIC boat.

(Below) U-751, a Type VIIIC boat, arrives in St. Nazaire, France in 1942. Returning submarines were customarily greeted by the staff of the U-boat service and Admiral Dönitz often attended the arrival cer-emonies. Most of the crew stands in formation on the after main deck. Only the engine and control room personnel are below deck, while most of the officers man the conning tower.

(Above) U-376 dispatches the 5,060 ton US merchant ship *Hoosier* in the Arctic Ocean on 10 July 1942. The ship was one of two Allied ships sunk by U-376 during the cruise.

(Right) The bow of U-757, a Type VIIC boat breaks the surface amid a torrent of depth charge explosions on 17 July 1942. The U-boat went down with 47 officers and men on board.

(Below) Warm and apparently friendly waters allow the crew of U-172 to relax before returning to the business of war. A FuMo 29 rigid radar array is mounted across the front of the conning tower. The antenna was normally protected by an environmental cover.

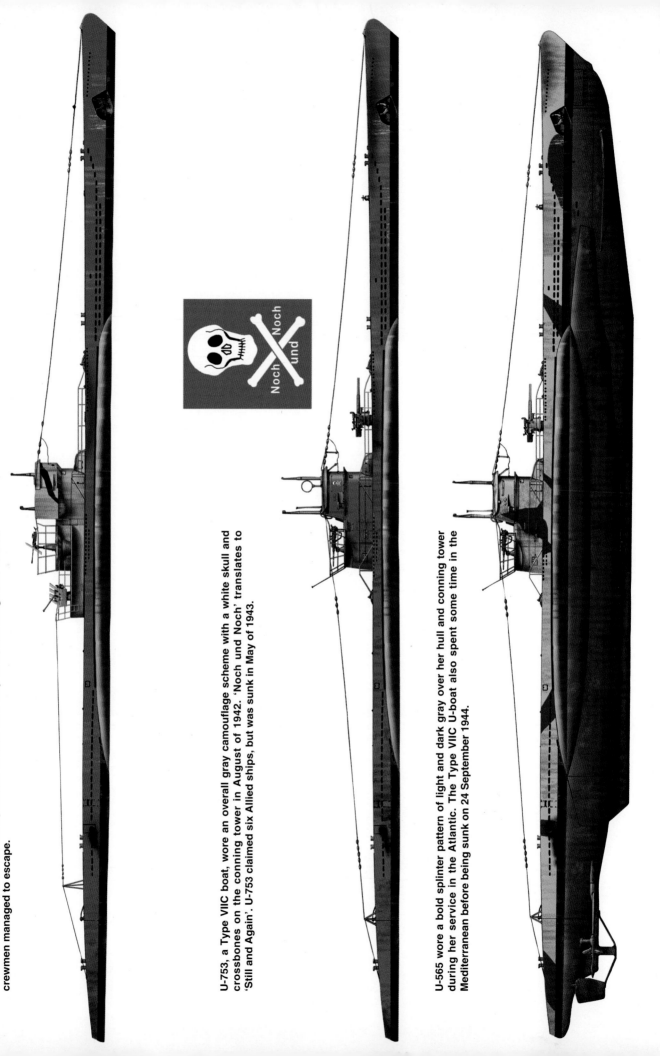

U-711 was a late war Type VIIC U-boat fitted with additional armor on the conning tower. The boat was commanded by Hans-Gunther Lange and spent most of her time operating out of Norway. U-711 was sunk by British aircraft on 5 May 1945, but Lange and several crewmen managed to escape.

U-753, a Type VIIC boat, wore an overall gray camouflage scheme with a white skull and crossbones on the conning tower in August of 1942. 'Noch und Noch' translates to 'Still and Again'. U-753 claimed six Allied ships, but was sunk in May of 1943.

U-565 wore a bold splinter pattern of light and dark gray over her hull and conning tower during her service in the Atlantic. The Type VIIC U-boat also spent some time in the Mediterranean before being sunk on 24 September 1944.

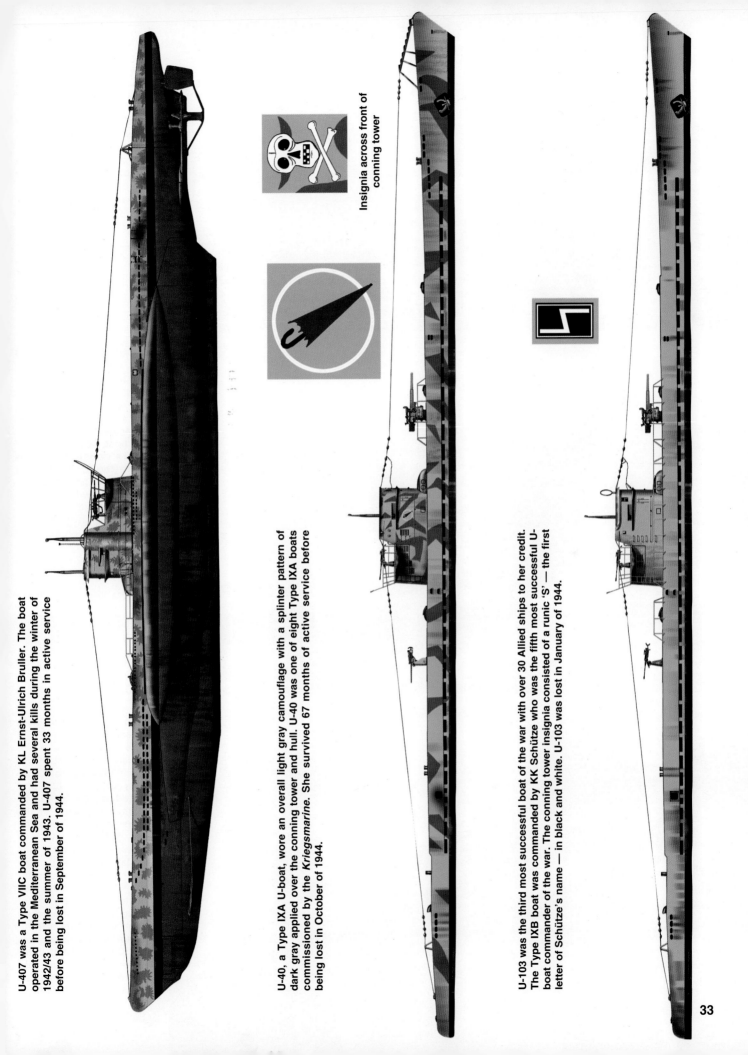

U-407 was a Type VIIC boat commanded by KL Ernst-Ulrich Bruller. The boat operated in the Mediterranean Sea and had several kills during the winter of 1942/43 and the summer of 1943. U-407 spent 33 months in active service before being lost in September of 1944.

U-40, a Type IXA U-boat, wore an overall light gray camouflage with a splinter pattern of dark gray applied over the conning tower and hull. U-40 was one of eight Type IXA boats commissioned by the *Kriegsmarine*. She survived 67 months of active service before being lost in October of 1944.

Insignia across front of conning tower

U-103 was the third most successful boat of the war with over 30 Allied ships to her credit. The Type IXB boat was commanded by KK Schütze who was the fifth most successful U-boat commander of the war. The conning tower insignia consisted of a runic 'S' — the first letter of Schütze's name — in black and white. U-103 was lost in January of 1944.

The 88mm deck gun is swung into action aboard U-172. The gunner aimed via a sight mounted on the side of the gun. Other crewmen loaded the gun and passed ammunition. The gun was an effective weapon, but fell into disuse as the war went on — many crews opting for additional flak weapons.

A WW II German post card commemorated the commissioning of U-352. The painting provides an excellent, and reasonably accurate view of the U-boat's lower hull. U-352 was a VIIC boat. Paintings of this nature concentrated on portraying the U-boats in an idyllic or heroic setting. Never seen were the horrors of a depth charging or a broken and flooding pressure hull plunging to the bottom.

U-234, a Type XB boat (left) sits alongside U-873, a Type IXD boat. U-873 appears to be a 'Milk Cow' which was designed to carry supplies, fuel and torpedoes for other U-boats. The ability of the 'Cows' to refuel and resupply U-boats at sea increased the boat's time on station and the number of attacks it could carry out. The 'Milk Cows' also offered the advantage of being able to submerge which made it more difficult to locate and destroy. The 'Cows' did not carry torpedo tubes, but did have deck and anti-aircraft guns for self-protection.

U-254, a Type VIIC boat, heads out on patrol on 8 August 1942. The boat was commanded by Hans Gilardone. Type VII boats were much smaller than Type IX submarines and formed the backbone of the Kriegsmarine's U-boat arm.

U-201 heads into port wearing a garland of leaves around the conning tower. The tower is decorated with two snow men which were the personal insignia Kapitän Adalbert Schnee (Snow). The life preserver, taken from one of the boat's victims, reads HMS T137. T137 may have been the *Shakesperian*-class trawler *Laertes* which was purchased by the Royal Navy, and sunk on 25 July 1942. The 88mm deck gun has been plugged with a waterproof tampion.

U-255, a Type VIIC boat, refuels a BV-138 seaplane at sea on 14 August 1942. The aircraft patrolled ahead of the boats and reported the position and defenses of convoys. Refueling the aircraft at sea increased their range and time on target. This type of operation also bred a close cooperation between the submariners and air crews. U-255 was commanded by KL Reinhart Reche. He commissioned the boat on 29 November 1941 and participated in the battle against convoy PQ 17. He was awarded the Knight's Cross on 17 March 1943 and shortly thereafter transferred to the staff of Commander U-Boats North.

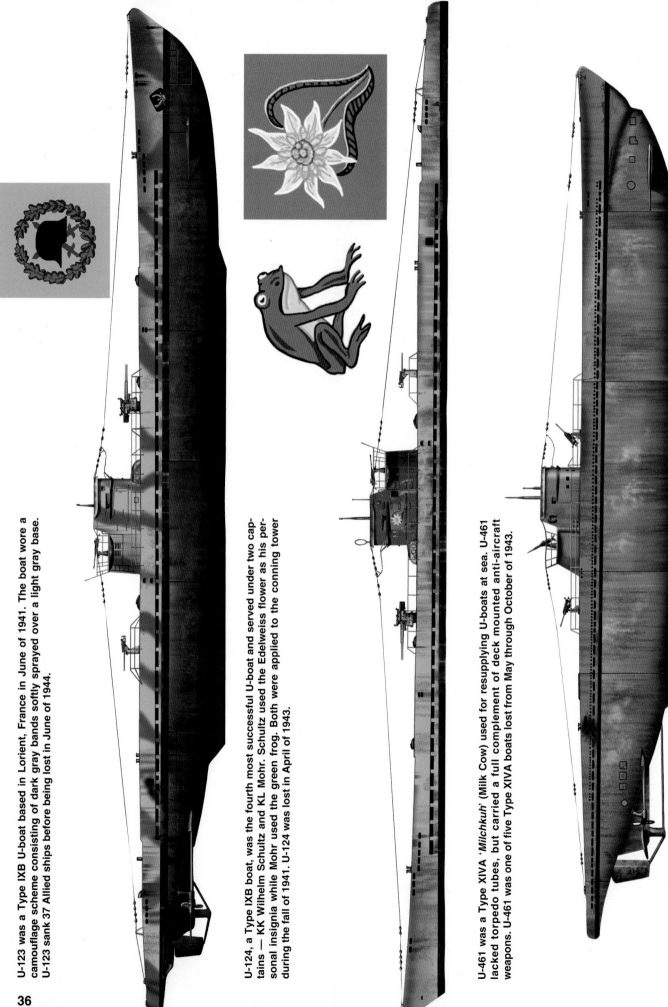

U-123 was a Type IXB U-boat based in Lorient, France in June of 1941. The boat wore a camouflage scheme consisting of dark gray bands softly sprayed over a light gray base. U-123 sank 37 Allied ships before being lost in June of 1944.

U-124, a Type IXB boat, was the fourth most successful U-boat and served under two captains — KK Wilhelm Schultz and KL Mohr. Schultz used the Edelweiss flower as his personal insignia while Mohr used the green frog. Both were applied to the conning tower during the fall of 1941. U-124 was lost in April of 1943.

U-461 was a Type XIVA 'Milchkuh' (Milk Cow) used for resupplying U-boats at sea. U-461 lacked torpedo tubes, but carried a full complement of deck mounted anti-aircraft weapons. U-461 was one of five Type XIVA boats lost from May through October of 1943.

This Type XXI U-boat was operational, but unidentified when it was photographed running on the surface during the last months of the war. The overall gray paintwork was heavily chipped and weathered.

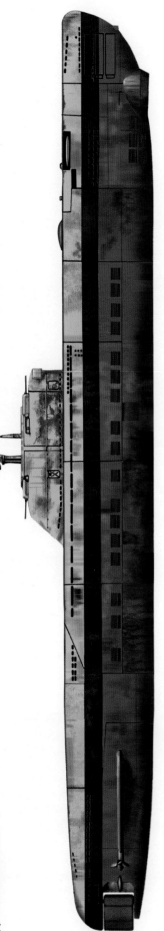

U-2502 was an operational Type XXI 'Elektro' boat under the command of KL Heinz Franke. It was surrendered to the British at the end of the war. Type XXI class boats were the largest combat boats in the Kriegsmarine inventory.

U-2321 was a one of a very few Type XXIII 'Elektro' boats put into commission before the end of the war in May of 1945. The boat carried a medium gray camouflage scheme with a light gray band and a white 'I' on the conning tower. U-2321 was commanded by Oberleutnant Hans-Heinrich Barschkis.

37

(Above) U-136 sits at pierside at St. Nazaire during the summer of 1942. The conning tower has an unusual camouflage scheme of dark gray diagonal lines over the light gray normally used on U-boats. The U-boat's crest is visible on the left of the tower.

(Below) U-132, a Type VIIC boat, was commanded by KL Ernst Vogelsang. The dark gray boat scored several success in the North Atlantic during June and July of 1942.

(Above) The bridge crew of U-109, a Type IXB boat, monitors docking activities after the boat returns from patrol. The bridge is wearing a disruptive camouflage scheme of light and dark gray. A 20mm antiaircraft gun is mounted on the platform behind the bridge. U-109 was commanded by KK Hans-Georg Fischer.

(Below) The crew of U-234, a Type XB boat, relaxes while in port. Although barracks ships were provided for U-boat crews, many preferred their own boats. This crew has set-up tables for lunch. The 88mm deck gun has been removed, leaving only the mounting plate and foot strips.

U-242

U-244

U-245

U-246

U-247

U-249

U-255

U-428

U-468

U-545

U-547

U-557

U-558

U-559

U-574

U-595

U-598

U-601 (a)

U-601 (b)

U-610

U-613

U-616

U-701

U-702

U-703

U-754

U-905

(Above) U-582, a Type VIIC boat, commanded by KL Werner Schultze returns from a successful mission in August of 1942. The American flag was taken from a US merchantman. The original caption on the picture noted the US merchant ship Stella Lykes was sunk at 0845 on 22 July 1942 and the Honolulu, another US vessel, was sunk later that day at 2012. The victory pennants are visible on the bridge periscope housing.

(Below) U-332, a Type VIIC boat, returns from patrol with her crew crowding the bridge and the 'wintergarten' as the aft flak platform was known. U-332 was commanded by KL Johannes Lieb who scored several kills in the North Atlantic during 1942.

(Above) The command group of U-201 guides the boat through the confined waters of a harbor. The officers and lookouts took positions where they could best observe and carry out their particular jobs. The barrel of the 20mm antiaircraft gun in the foreground has been removed and its socket plugged. U-201 was a Type VIIC boat.

The Tide Turns, 1943

Even as the U-boats headed out to the heavy seas of January of 1943, great changes were taking place within the leadership of the Kriegsmarine. On 31 December, German surface units had failed to press an attack on Convoy JW-51B and repeat the earlier success against Convoy PQ-17 during the previous July. Whether the failure was due to timidity, excessive caution, or simply happenstance is open to some debate. Nevertheless, a greatly displeased Adolph Hitler summoned *Grossadmiral* Erich Raeder, the Commander in Chief of the Kriegsmarine, and threatened to "throw the entire surface fleet into the dustbin". The arguments over the use of German capital ships (the battleship *Tirpitz* and the battlecruisers *Scharnhorst* and *Gneisenau)* resulted in Raeder's resignation as Commander-in-Chief on 30 January 1943. *Grossadmiral* Karl Dönitz was appointed as the new Commander-in-Chief of the Kriegsmarine. Admiral Hans-Georg von Friedeburg took over the responsibility as Admiral Commanding U-boats with authority over training, administration, and supply. U-boat combat operations were under the control of Dönitz's Chief of Staff *Konteradmiral* Eberhart Godt. The new appointments did not dramatically change the operation of the U-boats since Dönitz still maintained a strong interest in U-boat operations and the men he left in charge of the U-boat arm were trusted associates who had been with him for many years.

The U-boats were also a matter of grave concern in the Allied camp. At the Casablanca Conference (which began on 14 January 1943) the Allied leaders agreed that defeating the U-boats in the Atlantic was one of the primary concerns of military operations during 1943. Over a million men and millions of tons of supplies and equipment were moving across the Atlantic from the US to England in preparation for the invasion of Europe. It was vital that the men and supplies be protected from the U-boats. Indeed, the success of the invasion could not be guaranteed until the submarine threat was eradicated from the Atlantic Ocean. With

such impetus, the full weight of the Allied military machine swung into action against the U-boats. The men fighting the U-boats would get whatever equipment they needed. U-boat bases and construction yards would be primary targets of Allied strategic bombing and 80 long range aircraft would be allocated to the US Navy to close the gap in the Atlantic. Furthermore, the convoys would be accompanied by their own air cover in the form of small escort carriers carrying hunter-killer teams of aircraft. Convoys would now have air cover for the duration of their Atlantic crossing.

The first battle of the new year occurred on 11 January 1943 when eight U-boats, operationally known as the 'Delphin' Group, were sent against a convoy of tankers that had been located by German Intelligence. The boats located the tankers and sank seven of the nine ships in the convoy without loss. It was, however, to be one of the last successes for the U-boats.

Twenty U-boats located and massed against Convoy HX-224 at the end of January. The convoy was escorted by twelve warships and, in a two-day running battle the U-boats sank 13 out of 63 ships, but lost three of their own boats and had two others damaged. In fact the escorts had located and attacked 15 of the 20 U-boats at one time or another during the battle.

The engagement of Convoy HX-224 was just a portent of the climactic battles to come. By the beginning of February, *Grossadmiral* Dönitz had 409 U-boats on the rolls. Of these, 222 were operational and 178 were assigned to the Atlantic. The majority of these U-boats were formed into two large groups on either side of Atlantic Air Gap. The Germans were still unaware that the Allies had closed this gap and still believed they were safe from air attacks in this area.

During the early morning hours of 4 February 1943, a U-boat located Convoy SC-118 and reported its course and speed to Headquarters. The convoy had 64 merchantmen and was escorted by ten warships, several of which had the latest U-boat detection devices on board. Nineteen U-boats massed on the convoy, but they were constantly forced under by the alert escorts and long range patrol aircraft which seemed to be everywhere. Although the submarines eventually managed to sink ten of the Allied merchant ships, the U-boats lost three of their own and had

A bent and battered U-269 arrives in Bergen, Norway during 1943. The boat was commanded by Karl Heinrich Harlfinger and carried a coat of white camouflage paint. U-269 was a Type VIIC boat.

three other U-boats seriously damaged. Almost all of the submarines had been sighted and attacked by the escorts or aircraft during the battle. Three more large convoy battles followed in February. The Allies lost an average of 22% of the ships in each of these convoys, but Dönitz's U-boats were also suffering heavy losses.

The convoy battles spurred the Allied leaders to even greater action. Unhappy with the continued loss of valuable ships and supplies, the Allied military staffs met in Washington to better coordinate their efforts. The result was the creation of the US Tenth Fleet which provided a unified command to control all antisubmarine efforts in the Western Atlantic.

During the first eleven days of March, the Germans found and attacked four more convoys, sinking 23 ships. On 13 March German intelligence received information of three west bound convoys. Thirty-eight U-boats were alerted to the convoy's movements and deployed across the convoys' suspected track. Additionally, 13 other U-boats — which were in port — were refueled and sent out to reinforce the 38 submarines already on station.

The first contact with the convoys was made on 16 March when several patrolling U-boats discovered Convoy HX-229. U-603 was the first submarine to attack, firing a spread of the new FAT torpedoes against the merchant ships. The Germans did not know it but several of the U-boats which reported attacking HX-229, had in fact run into Convoy SC-122. One of the largest convoy battles of the war was underway.

The battle between the two Allied convoys and the wolf pack continued for five days. The U-boats sank 21 Allied ships amounting to 140,000 tons of shipping. Although the Germans heralded the battle as a great victory, it was in fact a disappointment. Had the wolf pack been truly effective it would have overwhelmed and destroyed both convoys. Over 50% of the submarines directed to engage the convoy actually located and attacked the convoy. Approximately 25 U-boats, in a target rich environment, were able to sink less than one Allied ship per boat. The poor showing was due to the increasing effectiveness of the Allied antisubmarine efforts. Aggressive escorts, coupled with constant air patrols, gave the German U-boat captains little time to line up an attack. Additionally, once the U-boat made an attack it was certain to be located by an escort or patrol aircraft. This forced the U-boat to dive deep and stay there while the convoy passed on. Few U-boats got off more than one attack which turned the odds in favor of the Allies.

Although the Germans sank a total of 779,533 tons of Allied shipping in March and new U-boats were being launched at a rate of 27 per month (most of these were Type VII boats), the defeat of the German submarine threat was close at hand.

Several new Allied antisubmarine measures were already taking effect. Allied air power assigned to the convoys was greatly increased at the end of March when three escort aircraft carriers were assigned to the Atlantic to hunt for submarines. Additionally, many of the Allied patrol aircraft were now equipped with the new ASV III airborne radar — a radar which could not be detected by the Metox radar warning system deployed on the U-boats.

The combined effect of the Allied antisubmarine efforts were felt in April of 1943 when the total tonnage sunk fell to half that achieved during the previous March. On 21 April nineteen U-boats located and attacked Convoy H-234. During four days of battle the Germans only sank two ships and the U-boats were in turn constantly attacked and harassed by the convoy's escorts.

In early May of 1943 the Germans made one last massive effort to overwhelm and destroy a convoy. A wolf pack of forty-one U-boats was directed against Convoy ON-55. The attack on the convoy began during the evening of 4 May and, over the next two days, the battle raged across the Atlantic. When the battle was over the Allies had lost 12 ships. The German U-boat arm, however, had paid a heavy price. Seven U-boats were sunk and five were badly damaged. A few other convoy attacks followed during the month, but it was evident that the Allied antisubmarine forces were now on the offensive. By the end of May twenty-two U-boats had been sunk and the Germans were forced to redeploy their U-boats to the less dangerous waters of the South Atlantic —a self defeating strategy since more Allied convoys and their cargoes

Crewmen, HQ Staff, yard workers, and families line the pier while U-405, a Type VIIC boat, is put into operation. The boat was commanded by KK Rolf-Heinrich Hopmann and scored several successes in the North Sea and Atlantic during the late winter of 1943.

U-407 wears a mottled camouflage scheme of irregular dark gray blotches over a light gray base . The lower half of the hull was usually painted red with a side black boot topping separating the colors. U-407 was under the command of KL Ernst-Ulrich Bruller. The boat had several successes while operating in the Mediterranean during the winter of 1942 and summer of 1943.

U-231, a Type VIIC boat, undergoes her final fitting out at the Kiel Navy Yard. The wooden structure is a form of camouflage and designed to emulate an innocent looking pier. U-231 enjoyed little success and was finally sunk in the North Atlantic while stalking Convoy SL 144. The U-boat was located by a Wellington bomber of No. 172 Squadron and sunk with depth bombs. Many of the U-boat's crew were rescued by an Allied escort vessel.

would arrive safely in England.

During the fall of 1943 and the first five months of 1944 the Germans lost 341 U-boats and over 20,000 experienced submarine crew members had been killed or captured by the Allies. While U-boat production was still ahead of losses, the replacement of crews — especially experienced crews that could stand up to the Allied onslaught — were impossible to find. The Battle of the Atlantic was all but over.

During the summer of 1944, with few U-boats to chase at sea, British Coastal Command sent its aircraft into the Bay of Biscay to attack the U-boats as they moved into and out of their ports. Armed with their new radar, the Allied aircraft were able to locate and sink several U-boats moving across the bay. Even when the aircraft failed to sink the submarine, their attacks and constant patrols kept the pressure on the U-boat crews already strained by continuous operations and the need to stay constantly alert while at sea. The 'happy times' of 1940, 1941, and early 1942 were a long forgotten memory among the German submariners.

In an effort to increase the lethality and survivability of the U-boats, German submarine designers and naval experts looked at new designs and added new technology to the existing U-boats. Work on a new radar detector that could pick-up airborne ASV III radar signals was begun. A bubble producing chemical agent was issued to the boats which could be launched to confuse enemy sonar. Two new types of U-boats, the **Type XXI** and **Type XXIII** were also put into production.

The Type XXI had a 1621 ton displacement and could cruise on the surface at 15.6 knots. It had an underwater speed of 17.2 knots, but could creep underwater at speeds of 2 to 3 knots for up to 500 miles. The Type XXIs were designed to stay deep even during an attack. The new U-boat could launch its torpedoes from a depth of 164 feet using hydrophones to zero in on the location of its target. Armed with acoustic homing torpedoes which homed in on the sound of a ship's propellers, all the submarine had to do was fire in the general direction of the target to insure a hit.

The Type XXIII displaced 232 tons, but had an underwater speed of 12.5 knots. It could cruise submerged for up to 110 miles and was extremely difficult to detect underwater. Both the Type XXI and XXIII boats would give the U-boat crews a better chance of survival if attacked since they could stay submerged long enough to endure the growing duration of Allied depth charging and make their escape.

The new U-boats also added the *Naxo* or *Timor* radar detectors to their arsenal. These detectors registered pulses between the 8cm and 12cm bands which was the range being used on new Allied airborne search radars. However, the apparatus only had a range of five miles — which was too short — and was prone to electrical failure. An effective radar detector, known as the *Fliege*, finally made its appearance during mid-1944, but too few of these sets reached the U-boats.

The German manufacturing firm IG Farben was also hard at work developing an outer coating for U-boat hulls that would absorb radar/sonar waves. This coating would allow the submarines to penetrate the Allied defensive screens without detection and sink enemy ships at will. However, the sophisticated coating was still new and untried and was subject to many teething problems.

The Germans also further developed the schnorkel. This device was a ventilating apparatus which allowed the boat to take in air for the diesel engines and the crew while still submerged. The net effect was that the submarine did not have to surface to air out the boat or recharge its batteries. Staying underwater, especially during daylight hours, considerably improved the boat's chance of survival.

Several tactical improvements were also added to the U-boats. The antiaircraft defenses were increased with the addition of a single 37mm antiaircraft gun in place of the quadruple 20mm mounts which had become popular on the U-boats. The 37mm weapon had a lower rate of fire, but had a greater range. Additionally, the larger shell had a greater effect on large Allied patrol aircraft. The weapon was also lighter than the 20mm quad mount. Nevertheless, the antiaircraft arrangement on the U-boats was often a matter of crew preference — many carried a pair of twin 20mm mounts in addition to either a 37mm or a quad 20mm weapon.

The Germans also continued to develop a new search radar for their U-boats. During early 1942 the Kriegsmarine had mounted modified gunnery radars on a few of the U-boats. These radars were fixed on the forward portion of the bridge and could locate targets out to 3.5 miles. However, the radar sets were not very effective since the boat had to sail in a complete circle to get 360 degrees of coverage. In August of 1943 a Luftwaffe 56cm *Funkmessortungsgerat* FuMo-61 was modified for use on submarines. The first set was fitted onto U-743 and proved quite effective and could detect targets out to 6.5 miles. It was ordered as standard equipment for U-boats after sea trials, but manufacture and delivery never kept up with demand.

While these technological developments offered great potential for the future, the U-boat war had to continue during the summer. Unable to stand up to Allied antisubmarine defenses in the Atlantic, the U-boats were redeployed along the African coast, the South Atlantic, and the Indian Ocean. The Allied antisubmarine defenses were not as strong in these areas and the U-boats soon made their presence felt. By the end of 1943 German submarines operating in the Indian Ocean had sunk 57 ships totaling 337,169 tons. These materiel losses were easily replaced by the Allies since few losses were being inflicted on the convoys plying the North Atlantic. In fact the U-boats sank only six ships in the Atlantic amounting to 23,000 tons in the month of November.

The year which had begun with such great hopes for the German submarines ended in disaster. The

U-528, a Type IXC boat, took part in the great North Atlantic convoy battles during the spring and early summer of 1943. U-528 was located near Convoy OS 47 on 11 May 1943 and sunk by a combination of Allied aircraft and escort vessels.

U-136 heads into a U-boat bunker at St. Nazaire, France. Each berth could hold two U-boats which completely protected them from marauding Allied fighters and bombers. U-136 was a Type VIIC boat.

U-404, a Type VIIC boat, loads torpedoes outside a submarine pen in France. One torpedo container is on the deck, while another has been angled into the loading chute.

U-boats had been driven out of the Atlantic shipping routes by the increasingly deadly and determined Allied antisubmarine forces. Allied aircraft were patrolling the entrances and exits to the German submarine bases and heavy bombers pounded the ports from the air. Most serious was the loss of over 20,000 experienced captains and crews which left the U-boat arm weakened and capable of only limited offensive action. Dönitz, however, knew that he could not abandon the war. If he did, great numbers of Allied ships, aircraft, and men — now being used to hunt U-boats — would be available for use against other portions the Third Reich. Even if the U-boats only scored occasionally, they would still tie down valuable Allied assets. The U-boat war would continue, perhaps with a sense of doom, into 1944.

U-703, a Type VIIC boat commanded by KL Heinz Bielfeld, rendezvous with a Blohm and Voss Bv 138C-1/U1 probably of 1 (F) SAGr 130 operating out of Trondheim. The aircraft provided a welcome way to deliver orders, mail, and other supplies to crews operating in northern waters. The fjords usually offered protected anchorages and enough space for the aircraft to land. A clip has been placed into the 20mm C/30 antiaircraft gun in the foreground.

U-235, a Type VIIC boat, mounted a heavier antiaircraft armament of a single 20mm cannon behind the bridge and a quad 20mm mount on the lower platform. Although an effective weapon, the quad 20mm mount's heavy weight interfered with the balance of the boat and its ability to perform emergency dives. This particular boat was sunk in Kiel harbor on 14 May 1943, but later raised and repaired. The boat was finally sunk — apparently by accident — by a German torpedo boat on 14 April 1945.

A returning Type VIIF U-Boat docks while the Captain issues docking orders via a megaphone. The crew waits in anticipation of a hot shower, hot food, and clean sheets on their beds.

'Naxos' Antenna

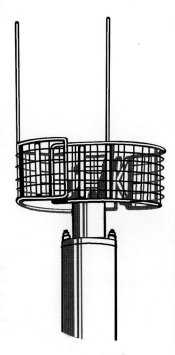

U-269 leaves harbor for another patrol. The boat was commanded by KL Harlfinger and operated in the North Atlantic and Mediterranean. The lack of any antiaircraft weapons is unusual. The boat may have been conducting an unusual experiment or undertaking a some sort of special mission.

U-873, a Type IXD boat, and U-234, a Type XB boat, are tied up at a quay. Mooring submarines side by side was common practice since their narrow beam easily allowed the two abreast arrangement.

(Above) U-172 is moved about a harbor by tugs. The U-boats were difficult to handle on the surface and tugs were often needed to maneuver the boat into and out of crowded ports. The Type IXC boat is characterized by her wide flat deck.

(Below) An RAF Coastal Command B-24 Liberator heads out over the Atlantic on patrol. These long range patrol aircraft closed the Atlantic Air Gap and helped end the U-boat scourge in the Atlantic. This particular version is armed with guns and British 3-inch rocket projectiles and carries radar (on the nose and under both wings) and a 24-inch Leigh Light under the starboard wing. (USAF Museum via Greg Sparh).

(Above) KL Klaus Bargsten of U-521 is escorted to a prisoner of war camp — believed to be Ft Eustis, Virginia. U-521 was sunk by the subchaser PC 565 on 2 June 1943 off the coast of Norfolk, Virginia.

(Below) U-614 was blown off her keel blocks after being caught in drydock during an Allied bombing raid on St Nazaire on 29 July 1943. The saddle tanks, underside, and rudder assembly are plainly visible. The boat was commanded by KL Wolfgang Strater. Strater had scored several victories while on patrol in the North Atlantic in February of 1943.

The crew of U-511, a Type IXC boat, hard at work on the bow of the submarine. The crewman are wearing their tropical dress uniform. U-511 carried Japanese Vice Admiral Nomura back to Japan during the summer of 1943. U-511 was commanded by KL Friedrich Steinhoff.

U-960 lies next to a German supply ship in September of 1943. The supply ship's camouflage helped it to blend into the land background as well as breaking up its outline at sea. German supply ships were hunted down and sunk wherever they were found, forcing the Kriegsmarine to resort to the less efficient *Milchkuh* boats.

The 'brain trust' of U-602 stands on the bridge while the boat eases into port. U-boat crews were small and each man had a well defined role to play in the operation of the boat. All the officers and crew realized the importance of being technically proficient at their jobs and the vast majority of crews functioned as a well oiled machine. The slightest mistake could result in loss of the boat or the death of the crew. KL Phillip Schuler stands out clearly on the bridge wearing his white hat cover and gloves. U-602 was a Type VIIC boat.

Eric Topp's U-552 arrives to a heroes welcome in a French port. The boat displays a bevy of victory flags and an obviously confident and happy command staff. Such jubilant welcomes became less frequent through 1943 since the U-boat loss rate began to climb as a result of improved Allied anti-submarine efforts.

2cm C/30 Flak

U-376 KL Freidrich-Karl Marks takes the salute of his crew amid a garland of leaves on the aft flak platform after returning from a successful patrol. KL Marks is standing on the 'wintergarten' — the conning towers after gun platform. This platform mounts a single 20mm Flak weapon.

(Above) Another WW II German post card shows three U-boats in port. The U-boat earned a heroic reputation during the war and such post cards were very popular among the German populace.

(Below) U-560, a Type VIIC boat, is tied up with several other submarines and a pair of subchasers. U-560 had little success at sea and was eventually damaged by the crew at Kiel on 3 May 1945 to keep it from falling into Allied hands in serviceable condition.

U-464, a Type XIVA supply boat, rides high, and likely empty, in port. The boat was one of only ten built during the war. Three were lost in a six day period in 1943. The greatest problem with the boats was the requirement to remain on the surface for an extended period while supplies, fuel and torpedoes were transferred. These U-boats were at a distinct disadvantage once the Allies closed the air gap in the North Atlantic and increased their aerial antisubmarine patrols.

U-460, a Type XIVA boat refuels U-135, a Type VIIC boat, in the foreground and another unidentified boat. The refueling line is running off the stern of U-460. While these resupply operations were initially successful, the Allied use of escort carriers and radar rendered the operations increasingly hazardous for all U-boat crews.

U-220, a Type XB U-boat, rides high in the water while in harbor. The amount of hull and superstructure visible while on the surface made the boat appear deceptively small. Much of the U-boat was below the water — much like an iceberg, but far more dangerous. U-220 was commanded by OL Bruno Barber and claimed two probable ships sunk in October of 1943.

(Left) Most U-boats were equipped with an 88mm or larger deck gun to dispatch smaller or crippled targets. This gun, named Spatz, is mounted on U-406, a Type VIIC boat. The gunner's sight and padded chest brace are mounted off to one side. It took an aimer, layer, and loader to man the gun. Additionally, three ammunition ratings brought ammunition to the gun. The large weapons gradually fell into disuse when Allied air power increased — the crews opting for additional Flak weapons.

(Below) Peter Erich Cremer's U-333 returns from patrol. Three victory pennants flutter from the periscope and the Kriegsmarine ensign waves from the jackstaff. The effects of patrol is evident in chipped paintwork on the conning tower. Both the 88mm deck gun and the after 20mm Flak mount, however, show little signs of wear and are ready for action.

(Right) U-960, a Type VIIC boat, moves in formation with another U-boat. The boat mounted a pair of twin-barreled Flak weapons on the aft conning tower platform. Boats entering and leaving port usually did so with an air and surface escort.

Biscay Cross Antenna

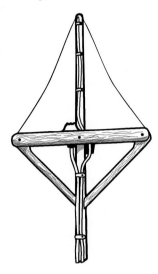

(Below) U-365, a Type VIIC boat, heads out for patrol amid the winter ice. The forward deck is awash, illustrating again how difficult a surfaced U-boat is to detect. The boat was commanded by KL Heimar Wedemeyer who scored several successes with the boat.

The Decline and End of the U-boat Arm, 1944- 1945

January of 1944 did not begin on a positive note. U-426 was sunk on 8 January as it crossed the Bay of Biscay and four other boats were damaged during the first week of the new year when they made their journey across the bay's open and increasingly perilous waters. The U-boat crews would not quit, however, even in the face of mounting and irreplaceable losses. Through much of January and February the Germans continued to harry the Allies with their submarines. There were seven operational boats in the Mediterranean, 33 in the Atlantic, four in the Black Sea, nine in the Indian Ocean, and 15 in the Arctic.

The U-boats achieved some successes in the Black Sea and Indian Ocean, but operations in the Atlantic were difficult at best. The boats rarely operated in wolf packs. The massing of U-boats simply presented the Allies with more targets. Instead, U-boat captains now launched individual attacks, choosing the most opportune time and place, and then making their escape before the Allied defenders could locate them. Attacks were augment by the use of the FAT torpedo which would run on a set course for a predetermined distance and then begin to zig zag. This allowed the torpedo a greater chance of hitting a ship in tight convoy formations. U-boats were also issued the improved **T5** *Zaunkonig* (wren) acoustic torpedo. This weapon homed in on the noise of propellers in the water and proved quite successful. However, even using these stealth tactics and improved torpedoes, the loss rate among the U-boats continued to climb. By February of 1944 eleven U-boats had been sunk along the convoy routes in the Atlantic and in return the boats had only sunk a single merchant ship. In the other oceans of the world the loss rate was somewhat better standing at one U-boat lost for each merchant ship sunk. The battle continued until April when many of the boats were recalled to defend the French coast against the impending Allied invasion.

In April of 1944 two new Type XIII boats were launched and a month later the first of the Type XXI U-boats slid down the ways. Dönitz had 448 U-boats at his disposal, but with the exception of the new boats and those older submarines equipped with schnorkels, the rest would not have much of a chance of getting near an Allied invasion fleet. Nevertheless, the U-boats still had to try to disrupt the invasion.

The U-boats assigned to striking the Allied invasion fleet were placed in two groups. Group *Landwirt*, assigned to attack an invasion fleet in the English Channel, was comprised of 49 Type VIIC boats stationed in Brest and St. Nazaire. The crews and boats were readied and placed on six hour notice. Twenty-one other boats, comprising Group *Mitte* were placed on alert in Norwegian ports in case the Allies tried to invade in the north.

None of the U-boats got near the invasion fleet. When the invasion was reported, eight schnorkel boats from Group Landwirt were directed to the main transport area and seven others were sent to Plymouth to destroy Allied shipping that was reinforcing the landings. Nineteen other U-boats established a defensive line along the Biscay coast. The Allied antisubmarine defenses, however, were at their best. U-413 was the first U-boat to run afoul of the Allied defenses. The U-boat was located and sunk on 7 June by a patrolling Allied aircraft. During the next two days three other Landwirt boats were sunk and six damaged when they tried to approach the invasion fleet. Only one of the Landwirt boats, U-162, actually reached the transport area. The U-boat sank a Tank Landing Craft, but was immediately attacked by a swarm of Allied escorts. The boat was driven to the bottom, but manage to creep away and actually survive the attack. Overall, the U-boats enjoyed little success and lost six of their own. The Germans continued to send U-boats against the invasion fleet in August — again without success — and lost a further three boats.

The loss of the French Atlantic ports in August of 1944 forced Dönitz to withdraw the U-boats from the French ports and redeploy them to bases in Germany and Norway. The move once again forced the Germans to use the northern passage into the Atlantic and the Allies quickly rerouted their convoys along routes which avoided the U-boats. During September, October, and November few merchant ships were sunk and only one U-boat was sunk. During the last four months of the year most of the U-boat activity was confined to the coastal waters around England. Only 24 Allied ships were sunk while the Germans lost 55 U-boats. Between June and the end of the year a total of 112 U-boats, along with most of their crews, had been lost — nearly 25% of the existing U-boat force.

U-423 carried a conning tower insignia and a unique two-tone paint scheme on her conning tower. The two-tone camouflage effectively reduced the ability of Allied escorts to visually detect the submarine on the surface. U-423 was a Type VIIC boat.

The Germans still had hope. In October the Germans had 37 Type XXI U-boats under construction, 13 fitting out, and 11 in commission. These boats had proven exceptionally difficult to detect during operational tests and their high underwater speed made them difficult to catch after their attacks. The Type XXIs, along with the smaller Type XXIII boats then under construction, offered the Germans one last chance to redress the balance of the submarine war in their favor — if enough of the boats could be built and deployed.

The Type XXI and XXIII U-boats were collectively known as *Elektro* boats and were given the highest construction priority. Dönitz believed he would have sufficient new boats, equipped with the latest search radar, protected by a radar/sonar absorbent coating, and carrying the most lethal torpedoes to reclaim the Atlantic as the U-boat hunting ground. Word of the new submarines and their capabilities, however, had reached the Allies and they spared no effort to bomb the production and transportation facilities which supported construction of the new boats. The Allies' fear that Dönitz could actually unleash these boats was so great that 80 Destroyer Escorts slated for the Pacific were retained in the Atlantic to counter the new U-boats if they made an appearance.

By early 1945 ninety of the new Type XXI and forty of the XXIII U-boats had been launched and were working up for operational patrols. Dönitz began the new year by quietly sending small groups of Type VII U-boats from Norway out into the waters north of the Shetlands. The boats were forced to use their Snorkels to avoid detection by Allied air patrols and thus, he had little communication with them. However, their orders were clear: locate and destroy enemy convoys using the northern convoy routes to England. The larger Type IX boats were sent on long range patrols to the South Atlantic, off the American coast, and the coast of Africa. None of the U-boats were detected on their outbound journey and January 1945 was one of the few months when a U-boat was not sunk by Allied escorts. The force was soon joined by the first of the Type XXI and XXIII boats which had departed Germany in February.

U-2511, a Type XXI commanded by KK Adalbert Schnee, scored well during the patrol sinking ten merchant ships totaling 45,000 tons. Several of the other boats also scored on this patrol and by March, an additional 39 U-boats were sent out to reinforce the attack group. The sudden increase of sinkings in the area drew the attention of the Allied antisubmarine forces. By the end of March eighteen U-boats had been

sunk and another 14 were obliterated while in port.

Despite the apparent success of the Type XXI U-boat, it was obvious to Dönitz that he would never be able to amass sufficient numbers of U-boats to retake the offensive. He realized that his U-boats were still tying down substantial Allied forces and, although he could do little else, he decided it was enough. The U-boat strength at sea grew to 61 by early April and Dönitz had a total strength on the book of 460 submarines. In April a further 44 boats put to sea, however, the end was near. Advancing Allied armies were forcing the evacuation of the U-boat construction and repair yards. On 25 April the advancing Soviet army forced Dönitz to move his Headquarters from Berlin to Kiel. On 2 May the advancing British army forced him to move his headquarters further north near Flensburg. The end came on 4 May 1945 when Dönitz issued an order to all Kriegsmarine ships and submarines to cease hostilities and return to base to surrender.

Although the U-boat captains had been ordered to surrender their boats, a total of 221 U-boats were scuttled by their crews between 4 and 8 May. A further 83 had been destroyed during the closing months of the war. Only 156 U-boats were actually surrendered to the victorious Allies.

The Germans built 1162 U-boats during World War II and manned them with 49,000 officers and men. Almost all of these boats had been used operationally. When the war ended and the losses totaled, the U-boats had sunk 4600 merchant ships totaling more than 21 million tons of shipping. U-boats also accounted for 175 Allied warships. Over 30,000 Allied sailors and merchant seamen were killed as a result of U-boat attacks. However, the cost had been high for the Germans as well. Seven hundred and eighty-five U-boats, along with 28,000 of their crews, were lost while on operational patrols. Another 5000 U-boat crewmen were taken prisoner during the war. By May of 1945 the Kriegsmarine's Gray Wolves had been virtually annihilated.

U-2513, a Type IXD, gently rolls in a calm sea off the US coast. This type of boat was developed as a long range resupply submarine and was an enlarged version of the IXC with its torpedo tubes and most of its batteries removed to make space for cargo. The Type IXD was equipped with more powerful diesel engines to give it a higher surface speed. This type was commonly called the Überseekuh (Overseas Cow) by the U-boat crews.

The conning tower watch of U-960 wears foul weather gear during less than perfect sailing weather. A single 7.9mm MG34 machine gun protects the tower. Such weapons were inadequate against heavier Allied aircraft. U-960 was commanded by OL Gunther Heinrich.

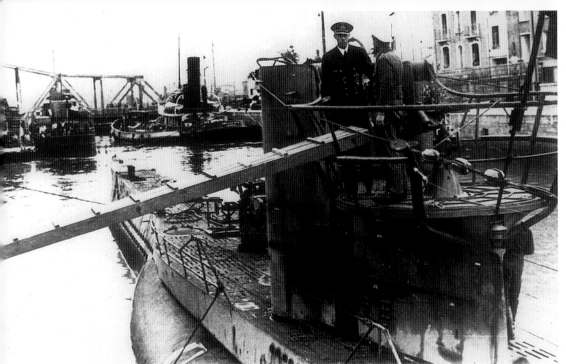

U-455 is tied up in port — possibly waiting for a visitor. Captain KL Hans-Henrich Giessler is wearing his dress uniform. The diminutive size of a U-boat often accounted for the unusual placement of gang planks, especially for distinguished visitors. U-455 had several successes In the North Atlantlc before being sunk with all hands on 6 April 1944.

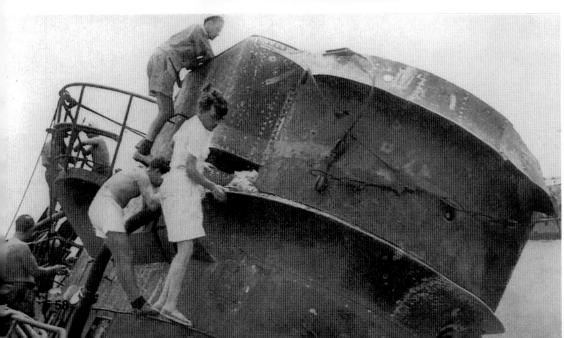

U-852 is examined by the British after it was beached along the coast of Somalia to keep it from sinking. Such captures were always important to the Allies, since they revealed the boat's technological strengths and weaknesses as well as their armament, electronics, and (occasionally) the all-important code books.

A FuMo 30 Centimetric radar with a rotating antenna was mounted on the conning tower of U-643. The radar set began to appear on U-boats during 1944 and was designed to detect ships as well as aircraft. U-643 is also equipped with the FuMo 29 radar located across the front of the conning tower. Five Olympic Rings are visible on the radar cover, signifying the Captain's Naval Academy graduation during the Olympic year of 1936. U-643 was a Type VIIC boat.

FuMo 30 Antenna

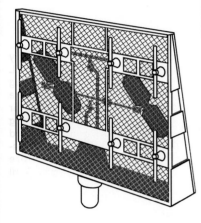

U-628, a Type VIIC boat, was equipped with a Metox set to detect enemy radar and the FuMo 29 rigid radar mounted on the forward portion of the conning tower. The FuMo 29 set was usually covered with a fairing. The addition of the radar, radar detectors, and heavier flak armament were an attempt to counter Allied submarine detection devices — especially those mounted in aircraft.

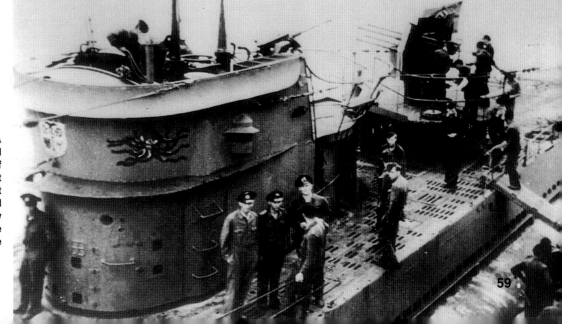

U-462, a Type XIV boat, sits in port. A 20mm 'flakvierling' has been added to the extended 'wintergarten' aft of the conning tower. The greatest drawback to the weapon was the fact that it was magazine fed and required constant attention from the gun crew to keep the guns loaded. U-462 wore a crest and octopus insignia on the conning tower.

(Left) U-307, a Type VIIC boat, cruises in calm water off Spitzbergen, Norway in 1944. The Type VIIC had a flare in the deck to provide additional working room for the deck gun crew. Twin 20mm Flak weapons are pointing skyward on the conning tower's after gun platform.

(Below) U-445 returns to port after a patrol. The jubilant crew stands at ease on the after deck while the officers stand ready on the 'winter garden'. Captain Graf Treuberg stands high on the bridge to ensure his boat is properly docked.

(Right) U-711, under the command of Hans-Gunther Lange, arrives in port after a patrol. The boat was a late war Type VIIC and is painted in a two-tone disruptive camouflage pattern of dark gray over light gray. A pair of twin 20mm mounts are visible behind the men on the bridge. Lange commissioned U-711 on 26 September 1942 and began his career by destroying the two Russian radio stations on the shore of the Petschora Sea. He operated against the Allied convoys on the Murmansk Run from his base in Norway. Lange torpedoed the Russian battleship Archangelsk at the end of 1941, but did not sink it. He was awarded the Knight's Cross on 26 August 1944 and the Oak Leaves on 29 April 1945. U-711 was sunk at Harstad by British aircraft on 5 May 1945, but Lange and several crewmen managed to escape.

(Below) U-462 rolls in the waves while refueling operations are underway. The refueling crew stands at ready while the look-outs scan the horizon for any sign of enemy aircraft or ships. U-462 was a Type XIV boat.

U-boats of the Kriegsmarine

Type I

Type IIC

Type VIIA

Type VIIB

Type VIIC

Type IXA

Type IXB

Type IXC

Type IXD

Type XIV

Type XXI

Type XXIII

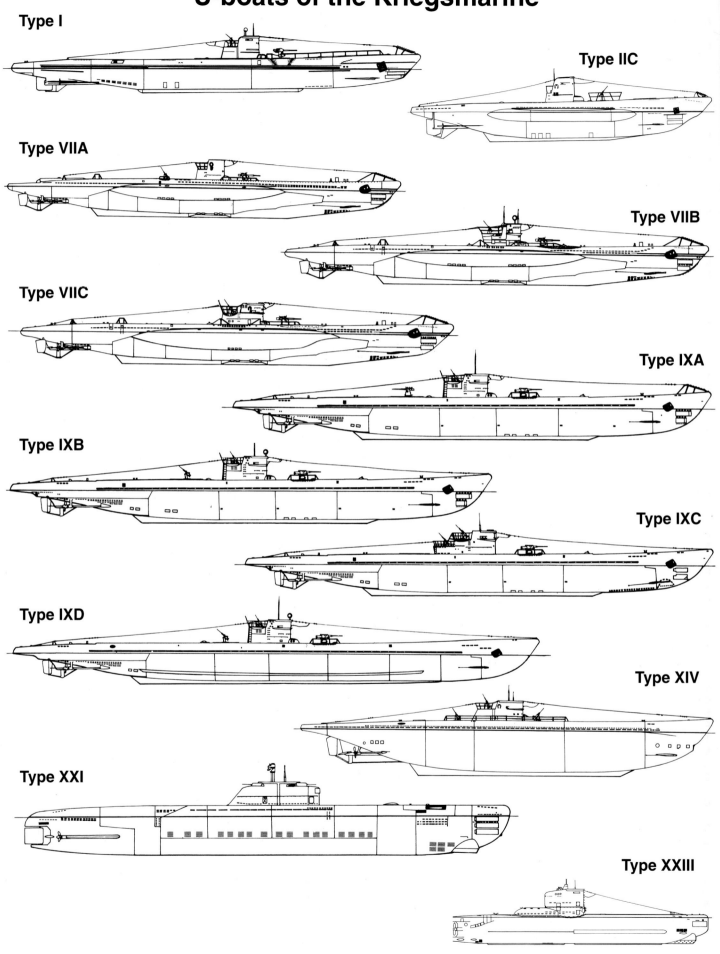

APPENDICES: THE U-BOAT WAR (1939-1945)

U-BOAT COMMAND STRUCTURE 1939
Commander in Chief of the Armed Forces. Adolf Hitler
Supreme Commander in Chief Navy. Erich Rader
Commander in Chief U-Boats. Karl Dönitz

U-BOAT FLOTILLAS

Number	Nickname	Base
1st	Weddigen	Germany; later in France
2nd	Salzwedel	Germany; later in France
3rd	Lohs	Germany; later in France
4th	None	Germany (Training Unit)
5th	Emsmann	Germany
6th	Hundius	Germany; later in France
7th	Wegener	Germany; France, and Norway
8th	None	Germany (Training Unit)
9th	None	France
10th	None	France
11th	None	Norway
12th	None	France
13th	None	Norway
14th	None	Norway
18th	None	Germany; formed in 1945 Probably for Type XXI and XXIII boats.
19th-27th	None	Germany (Training Units)
29th	None	France and Italy
30th	None	Black Sea
31st	None	Germany (Training Unit)
32nd	None	Germany (Training Unit)
33rd	None	Germany and Far East

TOP TEN U-BOAT CAPTAINS OF WWII

NAME	TONNAGE SUNK
Otto Kretschmer	314,000
Wolfgang Luth	253,000
Erich Topp	240,000
Gunther Prien	195,000
Herbert Schütze	185,000
Heinrich Lehmann-Wilenbrock	185,000
Victor Schultze	180,000
Karl Friedrich Merten	180,000
Heinrich Liebe	170,000
Georg Lassen	165,000

U-BOAT RANKS

Leutnant (L)	or Ensign
Oberleutnant (OL)	or Lieutenant JG
Kapitänleutnant (KL)	or Lieutenant
Korvettenkapitän (KK)	or Lieutenant Commander
Frigatekapitän (FK)	or Commander
Kapitän zur See (KS)	or Captain

GERMAN SUBMARINE TYPES	Type IA	Type II	Type VII	Type VIIA	Type VIIB	Type VIIC
Displacement (Sfcd/Submrgd in tons)	750/960	250/350	500/600	517/617	753/858	760/865
Length in feet	237.5	136.5	206.75	213.25	218.3	220.2
Beam in feet	20.3	13	19.3	19.75	20.3	20.4
Speed (Sfcd/Submrgd in knots)	20/9	13/7	16.5/8	16.5/8	17.25/8	17/7.5
Range @ 10 Knots	6,400	1,500	5,000 miles	5,000 miles	6,500 miles	6,500 miles
Torpedoes	6x21-inch	3x21-inch	5x21-inch	5x21-inch	5x21-inch	5x21-inch
Main Gun in mm	4-inch	1 pound	88mm	88mm	88mm	88mm
Diving Depth (Feet)	264	300	450	450	490	490
Complement	42	23	44	44	44	44

GERMAN SUBMARINE TYPES	Type IXA	Type IXB	Type IXC	Type IXD	Type XIV
Displacement	1032/1130	1051/1178	740/840	1616/1726	1690/1930
Length	251	250.9	244	287.5	220
Beam	21.4	22.3	21	24.6	30.25
Speed	18/7.5	18.2/7.3	18.2/7.3	19/7	15/6.5
Range @ 10 Knots	8,700	8,700	11,000	23,700	9,300 (at 12 kts)
Torpedoes	6x21-inch	6x21-inch	6x21-inch	6x21-inch	None
Main Gun	105mm	105mm	105mm	105mm	None (AA Weapons Only)
Diving Depth	400	490	490	400	360
Complement	48	48	44	57	53

GERMAN SUBMARINE TYPES	Types XXI	Type XXIII
Displacement	1621/1819	232/330
Length	251.7	112
Beam	21.7	12
Speed	15.6/17.2	9.5/12.5
Range @ 12 Knots	11,150	1,300
Torpedoes	6x21-inch	2X21-inch
Main Gun	4x20mm	None
Diving Depth	660	600
Complement	57	14

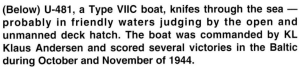

(Below) U-481, a Type VIIC boat, knifes through the sea — probably in friendly waters judging by the open and unmanned deck hatch. The boat was commanded by KL Klaus Andersen and scored several victories in the Baltic during October and November of 1944.

(Above) Surrounded by US ships and aircraft, U-505 is captured on the high seas off the coast of Africa. The aircraft, a Grumman TBF, and escort combination were the bane of all U-boats. U-505 is now a museum ship on display in Chicago, Illinois.

(Above) U-2524, one of the new Type XXI boats, is tied up at pierside during early 1945. Very few of these boats made it to sea before the war ended. The Type XXIs were designed to conduct most, if not all, operations while submerged. They were faster and quieter than any submarine in service at the time. Twin 20mm Flak turrets were mounted fore and aft in the conning tower.

(Left) A somewhat tattered looking Type XXIII boat, U2345, returns to port after a patrol. Only 59 of these diminutive 232 ton coastal boats were built before the war ended. Like the Type XXI boats, the Type XXIIIs were designed to conduct most operations while submerged. A boat of this type, U-2336, scored the last U-boat kill of the war.